SECULAR MARRIAGE, CHRISTIAN SACRAMENT

SECULAR MARRIAGE

CHRISTIAN SACRAMENT

Michael G. Lawler, Ph.D.

TWENTY-THIRD PUBLICATIONS
Mystic, Connecticut

Twenty-Third Publications
P.O. Box 180
Mystic CT 06355
(203) 536-2611

Library of Congress Catalog Card Number 85-51085
ISBN 0-89622-273-X

Cover design by George Herrick
Edited by Alice Fleming
Designed by Helen Coleman

In Thanksgiving For
Michael and Margaret Lawler,
My Parents

Foreword

Clearly, some shift is occurring in Roman Catholic understandings of the nature and the indissolubility of Christian marriage. While present theological reflection has been catalyzed by pastoral concern for the millions of Catholics who have been divorced, remarried, and consequently alienated from the Church, theology's task is not to fashion a practical pastoral procedure that will deal with this tragic situation—others have this responsibility. Rather, theologians are meant to study critically and carefully, with both honesty and openess, the centuries-long Christian tradition about "marriage in the Lord." This is what the present volume does.

Not surprisingly, the question of indissolubility proves to be a second-level question; the more basic issue is the nature of Christian marriage. What, if anything, is distinctive about Christian marriage as a sacrament? What is essential to it? What brings it into being? Michael Lawler has helped to sharpen these questions by pointing to the difference between a genuine human marriage that links two persons who happen to be baptized Catholics and a marriage between two Catholics in which their real faith and their appreciation of the *Christian* meaning of their union enters in as a component of their married relationship. What he has done in effect is to focus more sharply the question: what constitutes the sacramentality, and therefore the grounds of indissolubility, of a marriage between a Catholic man and woman?

Catholics are unaware that their Church's traditional teaching regarding marriage, divorce, and remarriage is not as clear and absolute as the Code of Canon Law, framed early in the 20th Century and recently revised, would have it. Indeed, the view of Christians over the centuries, even on the official level, have been far from clear and uniform. To that extent, it needs to be said—as Lawler says it—that the Code is a valuable but not completely adequate reflection of the faith and doctrine of the Church. It is possible, then, that the centuries-long tradition of the Church suggests greater pastoral flexibility than ecclesiastical legislation would indicate.

What this book, along with some other recent studies, is trying to do is not to find a way around the Church's faith and law, but to examine more carefully what Christian tradition has been with regard to the indissolubility of a sacramental marriage. Ultimately, the understanding and practical application of the indissolubility of Christian marriage will depend on the Christian community's understanding of the sacrament of Christian marriage; and this in turn will have to be a facet of the broader understanding of Christian sacramentality.

We are still a long way from grasping accurately what we mean by "Christian sacrament" or from understanding how that is to be applied to the context of human marriage. This book does not provide, nor does it pretend to do so, a worked-out explanation of the Christian sacramentality of a marriage between two believing Christians. It does little more than sketch, for example, the complicated history of theologians applying the term "sacrament" to marriage. What it does do is to establish the point that indissolubility is intrinsically linked to the sacramental dimension of marriage, that only in proportion to the actual sacramentality of a given marriage between two baptized Catholics can one speak of their union as "indissoluble."

While Lawler's stated objective is theological reflection on the indissolubility of Christian marriage, it is clear that he is pointing to the more fundamental, and ultimately more far-reaching, issue of the distinctiveness of Christian marriage as a sacrament. At a time in history when humans are becoming more explicitly conscious of personal relationships, when as a result there is wide questioning of the relationship between a woman and a man in marriage, it becomes critical for Christians to understand and live out the Christ-meaning of their union, so that by existing sacramentally they can reveal the deeper meaning of all human love.

Whether one agrees or disagrees with its arguments or its conclusions, this book should be listened to carefully. It forms part, and a professionally competent part, of a Roman Catholic discussion about marriage that has been long overdue. Lawler speaks honestly; he deserves to be heard honestly.

Bernard Cooke
Department of Religious Studies
College of the Holy Cross
Worcester, Mass.

Contents

SECULAR MARRIAGE, CHRISTIAN SACRAMENT

Introduction

In the early 1970s, the Roman Catholic diocese of Autun, France, initiated a marriage program that was radical in the modern Catholic church. A couple considering marriage was given a pamphlet which outlined three forms of marriage, and was asked to reflect on their own situation and to choose the form which corresponded best to it. The first form of marriage listed is *civil marriage*, a merely social marriage, registered with the state. The second form, which follows a civil marriage, is *welcomed civil marriage*, a celebration which takes place, perhaps, at home, in the church, in the town hall, but always with some sort of church setting. The civilly married couple, who have stated that they do not believe in sacramental marriage but still wish to solemnize their commitment to one another in some sort of a religious ceremony, are welcomed by the gathered church, which proclaims its own faith in Christian marriage through the lives of the married couples gathered for the welcoming. The third form of marriage is *sacramental marriage*, celebrated by those couples who, in Christian faith, wish their marriage to be an explicit symbol of the covenant union between Christ and his Church. Couples who are not yet ready for sacramental marriage may celebrate the first two forms and, later, following a catechumenate-like period of reflection to deepen their personal faith, a sacramental marriage.[1]

The impetus for the establishment of this program was provided by the many requests for a church wedding made by *baptized nonbelievers*, that is, men and women who had been baptized at some time in their lives, usually in infancy, but had never been nurtured by Christian faith.[2] According to the long-established theological tradition of the Catholic Church, such nonbelievers, of which there are many in France, and probably just as many in the Americas, are not in a position to enter into a genuinely *Christian* marriage. Every Christian sacrament, the church has always taught, requires personal faith for its validity and fruitfulness. The Autun program was established to demonstrate the church's concern for nominal, nonbelieving Catholics. Through the program, the diocese of Autun, along with several other dioceses in France, acknowledges the validity of a genuinely human marriage,

1

welcomes such a marriage, and nurtures nominal believers into a faith which makes possible a thoroughly sacramental Christian marriage.

A major problem with this program, and therefore a source of most of the objections to it, was that it took up a theological position at variance with the legal position taken by the *Code of Canon Law.* Canon 1012 of the 1917 *Code* stated: 1) Christ the Lord raised the contract of marriage between baptized persons to the dignity of a sacrament; 2) therefore, a valid marriage contract cannot exist between baptized pesons without being, by that very fact, a sacrament. The same position was restated essentially in Canon 1055 of the revised 1983 *Code.* The Autun program directors and many Roman Catholic theologians are in full agreement with the *Code* when it states that the universal secular institution of marriage is sometimes also a Christian sacrament. They are in open disagreement with it, however, when it claims that the universal secular institution of marriage, when celebrated between two persons who have been baptized, is *always* a Christian sacrament. There is a substantial difference, they believe, between valid secular marriage and valid Christian marriage, a difference created by genuine Christian faith. The law of the church, they further believe, is simplistic and quite unrealistic when it equates the two in the case of those who have been baptized.

I focus on the Autun program to draw attention to one outstanding problem in the now-traditional theory and practice of Christian marriage in the Roman Catholic Church and to set in relief one divergence between traditional Roman Catholic theology and traditional Roman Catholic law. This book, which seeks to articulate a contemporary Roman Catholic theology of Christian marriage, will return to this problem again and again.

Marriage, of course, is a universal human institution. As such it antedates Christianity, and consequently must have humanly satisfying meaning apart from Christian sacrament. In this book I deal with marriage not in all of the many facets of the human community, but exclusively the facet existing in the Christian religious community. I will consider the difference between merely secular marriage and Christian sacramental marriage; the circumstances in which secular marriage is transformed into Christian marriage; and the implications of such a transformation for living a thoroughly human and Christian life.

Christians, like all other women and men, are born into the world naked, but they are not born into a naked world. They are born into a world that is replete with meanings for things, including marriage, that men and women value and hold as crucial in their human lives. Such meaning constitute what is known in the secular world as culture and what is known in the religious world as tradition. That is not to suggest, of course, that the secular world and the religious world are quite separate realities, for they are not. But neither are they identical worlds, and they should never be treated as such. It is this mistake, I shall argue, that the *Code of Canon Law* and the practice that derives from it make.

I will demonstrate throughout this book the distinction between secular marriage and Christian marriage. The distinction is one between everyday reality and a deeper, mysterious reality. It is the distinction between a square of cloth and a flag, between a lump of metal and a wedding ring, between immersion in water, and the celebration of death and resurrection, between mating and making love, between sharing a meal together and making the Body of Christ. I shall argue that as sometimes women and men can relate to a square of cloth but not a flag, a meal but not the Body of Christ, mating but not making love, so also can they relate, be they ever so baptized, to secular marriage but not to Christian marriage, the symbol-sacrament of the covenant union between Christ and his Church.

The book analyzes the tradition of Christian marriage as it emerges from the Christian Scriptures (chapter one) and the ongoing Christian Church (chapter two). It seeks to uncover the very essence of Christian marriage as it has been articulated in the Roman Catholic tradition down to our day (chapter three). It seeks, further, to elaborate a contemporary Roman Catholic theology of Christian marriage, explicating precisely the meaning of secular marriage that is sometimes also Christian sacrament (chapter four). Finally, recognizing with the Christian Churches the sad reality that Christians sometimes fail in marriage, the book confronts the painful situation of many Christians who are divorced and remarried, and seeks out compassionate pastoral approaches to them.

I am a married theologian in the Roman Catholic Church. I enjoy the freedom enjoyed by a theologian in that church, a freedom which I confess gladly is not an unlimited freedom, but one that is bound to both truth and "the moral principle of personal and social responsibility."[3] A theologian makes neither the doctrine or the law of his church. His task is a less lofty one. It is the task "of interpreting the documents of the past and present magisterium, of putting them in the context of the whole of revealed truth, and of finding a better understanding of them by the use of hermeneutics." It is a task that "brings with it a somewhat critical function," which I am happy to acknowledge should "be exercised positively rather than destructively."[4] It is as a positively constructive interpretation and updating of the Catholic tradition that I offer this work.

Every author experiences myriad influences, and I confess that I am no exception. Those who have influenced this book will recognize their effects and, I trust, be happy for it.

I dedicate this book to all Christian wives and husbands, some of them divorced and some of them remarried, who forced me to reflect on the uniqueness of Christian marriage. But I dedicate it especially to my parents, the wife and husband who first exemplified for me the distinctive nature of matrimony in the Catholic Church.

I would also like to acknowledge with gratitude a research grant from the Graduate School of Creighton University that made the early completion of this book possible.

Marriage in the Bible

As in all other matters, the Biblical teaching on marriage should be seen in the context of the Near Eastern cultures with which the people of the Bible had intimate links, specifically the Mesopotamian, Syrian, and Canaanite. It is not my intention here to dwell on these cultures and their teachings on marriage and sexuality. They were all quite syncretistic, and a general overview sufficiently gives both a sense of the context and their specific distinctions from the Jewish Bible.

Underlying the themes of sexuality, fertility, and marriage in these cultures are the archetypal figures of the god-father and the goddess-mother, the sources of universal life in the divine, the natural, and the human spheres. Myths celebrated the marriage, the sexual intercourse, and the fertility of this divine pair, legitimating the marriage, the intercourse, and the fertility of every earthly pair. Rituals acted out the myths, establishing a concrete link between the divine and the earthly worlds and enabling men and women to share not only in the divine action but also in the efficacy of that action. This is especially true of sexual rituals, which bless sexual intercourse and ensure that the unfailing divine fertility is shared by man's plants and animals and wives, all important elements in his struggle for survival in those cultures[1]. In Mesopotamia, the divine couple is Ishtar and Tammuz; in Egypt, Isis and Osiris; in Canaan, Ashtarte (or Asherah) and, sometimes, Eshmun. After the Hellenization of Canaan, Eshmun is given the title of Adonis.

Marriage in the Old Testament

The Biblical view of sexuality, marriage, and fertility makes a radical break with this polytheistic perspective. The Old Testament, whose view of marriage I do not intend to treat fully here but only as it provides the basis for the New Testament view of Christian marriage, does not portray a god-goddess couple, but only Yahweh who led Israel out of Egypt and is unique (Deuteronomy 6:4). There is no goddess associated with him. He needs no goddess, for he creates by his word alone. This God created man and woman, "male and female he created them and he named *them 'adam*" (Genesis 5:2). This fact alone, that God names male and female together *'adam* (that is, earthling or humankind), founds the equality of man and woman as human beings, whatever be their distinction in functions. It establishes them as "bone of bone and flesh of flesh" (Genesis 2:23), and enables them "therefore" to marry and to become "one body" (Genesis 2:24). These details are taken from the early Yahwist creation account. But the much later priestly account which we find in Genesis 1 also records the creation of male and female as *'adam* and the injunction given them to "be fruitful and multiply and fill the earth" (Genesis 1:28).

Equal man and woman, with their separate sexualities and fertilities, do not derive from a divine pair whom they are to imitate. They are called into being by the creative action of the sovereign God. Man and woman *'adam*, their sexuality, their marriage, their fertility are all good, because they are the good gifts of the Creator. Later Christian history, as we shall see, will have recurring doubts about the goodness of sexuality and its use in marriage, but the Jewish Biblical tradition had none. As gifts of the Creator God, who "saw everything that he had made and behold it was very good" (Genesis 1:31), sexuality, marriage, and fertility were all good, and belonged to man and woman as their own, not as something derived from some divine pair. When looked at within this context of creation-gift, all acquired a deeply religious significance in Israel. That is not to say that they were sacred in the sense in which the fertility cults interpreted them as sacred, namely, as participation in the sexuality and sexual activity of the divine pair. In that sense they were not sacred, but quite secular. But in another sense, the sense that they were from God and linked man and woman to God, they were both sacred and religious. "It was not the sacred rites that surrounded marriage that made it a holy thing. The great rite which sanctified marriage was God's act of creation itself."[2] It was God alone, unaided by any partner, who not only created 'adam with sexuality and for marriage but also blessed him and them, thus making them inevitably good.

Man and woman together are named 'adam. They are equal in human dignity and complementary to one another; there is no full humanity without both together. Human creation, indeed, is not complete until they stand together. It is precisely because man and woman are equal, because they are 'adam, because they are "bone of bone and flesh of flesh," that is, because they share human strengths and weaknesses, that they may marry and become "one body"(Genesis 2:24). Among the birds of the air and the animals of the field there "was not found a helper fit" for the man (Genesis 2:20), and it is not difficult to imagine man's cry of delight when confronted by woman. Here, finally, was one who was his equal, one whom he could marry and with whom he could become one body.

That man and woman become one body in marriage has been much too exclusively linked in the Western tradition to one facet of marriage, namely, the genital. That facet is included in becoming one body, but it is not all there is. For *body* here implies the entire person. "One personality would translate it better, for 'flesh' in the Jewish idiom means 'real human life.' "[3] In marriage a man and a woman enter into a fully personal union, not just a sexual or genital one. In such a union they become one person, one life, and so complement one another that they become 'adam. They enter into a union which establishes not just a legal relationship, but a blood relationship which makes them one person. Rabbis go so far as to teach that it is

what is the use of person here?,

only after marriage and the union of man and woman into one person that the image of God may be discerned in them. An unmarried man, in their eyes, is not a whole man.[4] And the mythic stories,[5] interested as always in aetiology, the origin of things, proclaim that it was so "in the beginning," and that it was so by the express design of God. There could be for a Jew, and for a Christian, no greater foundation for the human and religious goodness of sexuality, marriage, and fertility. Nor could there be a secular reality better than marriage for pointing to God and his steadfastly loving relationship with Israel. That was the next step in the development of the religious character of marriage.

Marriage as Covenant Symbol

Central to the Israelite notion of their special relationship with God was the idea of the covenant. The Deuteronomist reminded the assembled people: "You have declared this day concerning Yahweh that he is your God and Yahweh has declared this day concerning you that you are a people for his own possession" (Deuteronomy 26: 17-19). Yahweh is the God of Israel; Israel is the people of Yahweh. Together Yahweh and Israel form a community of grace, a community of salvation, a community, one could say, of one body. It was probably only a matter of time until the people began to imagine this covenant relationship in terms drawn from marriage, and it was the prophet Hosea who first did so. He preached about the covenant relationship of Yahweh and Israel within the biographical context of his own marriage to a harlot wife, Gomer. To understand his preaching, about marriage and about the covenant, we must first understand the times in which Hosea lived.

Hosea preached around the middle of the eighth century B.C., at a time when Israel was well established in Canaan. Many Israelites thought that the former nomads had become too well established in their promised land, for as they learned their new art of agriculture they learned also the cult of the Canaanite fertility god, Baal. This cult, which seriously challenged their worship of Yahweh, was situated in the classic mold presented earlier, that of the god-goddess pair, with Baal as the Lord of the earth and Anat as his wife (and sister). The sexual intercourse and fertility of these two were looked upon as establishing the pattern both of creation and of the fertile intercourse of every human pair. The relationship of human intercourse and its fertility to that of the divine couple was acted out in temple prostitution, which required both *kedushim* and *kedushoth*, that is, male and female prostitutes. These were prohibited in the cult of Yahweh (Deuteronomy 23:18), and any Jewish maiden participating in temple prostitution was regarded as a harlot. It was such a harlot, Gomer, that Hosea says Yahweh instructed him to take for his wife (1:2-3).

It is quite irrelevant to the present discussion whether the book of Hosea tells us what Hosea did in historical reality, namely, took a harlot-wife and remained faithful to her despite her infidelity to him, or whether it offers a parable about marriage as steadfast covenant. What is relevant is that Hosea found in marriage, either in his own marriage or in marriage in general, an image in which to show his people the steadfastness of Yahweh's covenantal love for them. On a superficial level, the marriage of Hosea and Gomer is just like any other marriage. But on a more profound level, it serves as prophetic symbol, proclaiming and realizing and celebrating in representation the covenant relationship between Yahweh and Israel.

The names of Hosea's two younger children reflect the sad state of that relationship: a daughter is Not Pitified (1:6), and a son is Not My People (1:9). As Gomer left Hosea for another, so too did Israel abandon Yahweh in favor of Baal and become Not Pitied and Not My People. But Hosea's remarkable reaction proclaims and makes real in representation the remarkable reaction of Yahweh. He buys Gomer back (3:2); that is, he redeems her. He loves her "even as Yahweh loves the people of Israel, though they turn to other gods" (3:1). Hosea's action towards Gomer reveals and makes real in representation the action of Yahweh's unfailing love for Israel. In both cases, that of the human marriage symbol and of the divine covenant symbolized, the one body relationship had been placed in jeopardy. But Hosea's posture both is modeled upon and models that of Yahweh. As Hosea has pity on Gomer, so Yahweh "will have pity on Not Pitied," and will "say to Not My People 'you are my people,'" and they will say to him, "Thou art my God" (2:23). The covenant union, that between Hosea and Gomer as well as that between Yahweh and Israel, is restored. A sundering of the marital covenant relationship is not possible for Hosea because he recognized that his God is not a God who can abide the dissolution of covenant, no matter what the provocation. He believed what the prophet Malachi would later proclaim: "I hate divorce, says Yahweh, the God of Israel . . . so take heed to yourselves and do not be faithless" (2:16).

There are two possibilities of anachronism to be avoided here. The first is that overworked word *love*. In its contemporary usage, it always means a strong affection for another person, frequently a passionate affection for another person of the opposite sex. When we find the word in our Bible it is easy to assume that it means the same thing. But it does not. Covenant Love, of which Hosea speaks and which we read of first in Deuteronomy 6:5, is not a love of interpersonal affection but a love that is "defined in terms of loyalty, service and obedience."[6] When we read, therefore, of Hosea's steadfast love for Gomer and of Yahweh's faithful love for Israel, we ought to understand loyalty, service and obedience, and not interpersonal affection. The second possibility of anachronism rests in the hatred of divorce proclaimed by Malachi. "In the circumstances addressed by Malachi, what God hates is the divorce of Jew and Jew; there is silence about the divorce of Jew and non-Jew."[7] The post-exilic reforms of Ezra and Nehemiah require the divorce of all non-Jewish wives and marriage to Jewish ones. Malachi speaks for this period. The divorce of Jewish wives is hated, but the divorce of non-Jewish ones is obligatory. As we shall see, Paul will adapt this strategy to the needs of his Corinthian church, and it continues to be a crucial factor in the Catholic strategy toward divorce in our day.

What ought we to make of the story of his marriage that Hosea leaves to us? There is a first, and very clear, meaning about Yahweh: he is faithful. But there is also a second, and somewhat more mysterious, meaning about human marriage: not only is it the loving union of a man and a woman, but it is also a prophetic symbol, proclaiming and making real in representative image the steadfast love of Yahweh for Israel. First articulated by the prophet Hosea, such a view of marriage recurs again in the prophets Jeremiah and Ezekiel. Ultimately, it yields the view of Christian marriage that we find in the New Testament.

Both Jeremiah and Ezekiel present Yahweh as having two wives, Israel and Judah (Jeremiah 3:6-14), Oholah-Samaria and Oholibah-Jerusalem (Ezekiel 23:4). Faithless Israel is first "sent away with a decree of divorce" (Jeremiah 3:8), but that does not deter an even more faithless Judah from "committing adultery with stone and tree" (Jeremiah 3:9). Israel and Judah are as much the harlots as

Gomer but Yahweh's faithfulness is as unending as Hosea's. He offers a declaration of undying love: "I have loved you with an everlasting love; therefore, I have continued my faithfulness to you" (Jeremiah 31:3; cf. Ezekiel 16:63; Isaiah 54:7-8). The flow of meaning, as in Hosea, is not from human marriage to divine covenant, but from divine covenant to human marriage. The belief in and experience of covenant fidelity creates the belief in and the possibility of fidelity in marriage, which then and only then becomes a prophetic symbol of the covenant. Yahweh's covenant fidelity becomes a characteristic to be imitated, a challenge to be accepted, in every Jewish marriage. Malachi, as we saw already, puts it in a nutshell: "I hate divorce, says Yahweh . . . so do not be faithless" (2:16).

Marriage in the New Testament

The conception of marriage as a prophetic symbol, a representative image of a mutually faithful covenant relationship is continued in the New Testament. But there is a change of *dramatis personae*, from Yahweh--Israel to Christ--Church. Rather than presenting marriage in the then-classical Jewish way as an image of the covenant union between Yahweh and Israel, the writer of the letter to the Ephesians[8] presents it as an image of the relationship between the Christ and the new Israel, his church. This presentation is of such central importance to the development of a Christian view of marriage and unfortunately has been used to sustain such a diminished Christian view that we shall have to consider it here in some detail.

The passage in which the writer offers his view of marriage (5:21-33) is situated within a larger context (5:21-6:9) which sets forth a list of household duties that exist within a family at that time. This list is addressed to wives (5:22), husbands (5:25), children (6:1), fathers (6:4), slaves (6:5) and masters (6.9). All that concerns us here is, of course, what is said of the pair, wife/husband. There are two similar lists in the New Testament, one in the letter to the Colossians (3:18-4:1), the other in the first letter of Peter (2:13-3:7). But the Ephesians' list is the only one to open with a strange injunction. "Because you fear Christ subordinate yourselves to one another;"[9] or "give way to one another in obedience to Christ;"[10] or, in the weaker translation of the Revised Standard Version, "be subject to one another out of reverence for

Christ."[11] This injunction, most commentators agree, is an essential element of what follows.

The writer takes over the household list from traditional material, but critiques it in 5:21. His critique challenges the absolute authority of any one Christian group over any other, of husbands, for instance, over wives, of fathers over children, of masters over slaves. It establishes a basic attitude required of all Christians, an attitude of giving way or of mutual obedience, an attitude which covers all he has to say not only to wives, children, and slaves, but also to husbands, fathers, and masters.[12] Mutual submission is an attitude of all Christians, because their basic attitude is that they "fear Christ." That phrase probably will ring strangely in many ears, clashing with the deeply rooted Augustinian-Lutheran claim that the basic attitude toward the Lord is not one of fear, but of love. It is probably for this reason that the Revised Standard Version rounds off the rough edge of the Greek *phobos* and renders it as *reverence* . But *phobos* does not mean reverence. It means fear, as in the Old Testament aphorism: the fear of the Lord is the beginning of wisdom (Proverbs 1:5; 9:10; 15:33; Psalms 111:10).

The apostle Paul is quite comfortable with this Old Testament perspective. Twice in his second letter to the Corinthians (5:11 and 7:1) he uses the phrase *fear of God* . In his commentary on Ephesians, Schlier finds the former text more illuminating of Ephesians 5:21.[13] But I am persuaded, with Sampley, that the latter is a better parallel.[14] Second Corinthians 6: 14-18 recalls the initiatives of God in the covenant with Israel and applies these initiatives to Christians, who are invited to respond with holiness "in the fear of God" (7:1). The fear of God that is the beginning of wisdom is a radical awe and reverence that grasps the mighty acts of God and responds to them with holiness. In 2 Corinthians 6:14-17 that holiness is specified as avoiding marriage with unbelievers; in Ephesians 5:21 it is specified as giving way to one another. That mutual giving way is required of all Christians, even of husbands and wives as they seek holiness together in marriage, and even in spite of traditional family relationships which permitted husbands to lord it over their wives.

As Christians have all been admonished to give way to one another, it comes as no surprise that a Christian wife is to give way to her husband, "as to the Lord" (5:22). What does come as a surprise, at least to the ingrained male attitude that sees the husband as supreme lord and master of his wife and appeals to Ephesians 5:22-23 to ground and sustain that un-Christian attitude, is that a husband is to give way to his wife. That follows from the general instruction that Christians are to give way to one another. It follows also from the specific instruction about husbands. That instruction is not that "the husband is the head of the wife" (which is the way in which males prefer to read and cite it), but rather that "in the same way that the Messiah is the head of the church is the husband the head of the wife."[15] A Christian husband's headship over his wife is in image of, and totally exemplified by, Christ's headship over the Church. When a Christian husband understands this, he will understand the Christian responsibility he assumes toward the woman-gift he receives in marriage as his wife. In a Christian marriage, spouses are required to give way mutually, not because of any inequality between them, not because of any subordination of one to the other, not because of fear, but only because they have such a personal unity that they live only for the good of that one person. Mutual giving way, mutual subordination, and mutual obedience are nothing other than total availability and responsiveness to one another so that both spouses can become one body.

The way Christ exercises headship over the church is set forth unequivocally in Mark 10:45: "The Son of Man came not to be served but to serve, and to give his life as a ransom (redemption) for many." *Diakonia*, service, is the Christ way of exercising authority, and our author testifies that it was thus that "Christ loved the church and gave himself up for her" (Ephesians 5:25). A Christian husband, therefore, is instructed to be head over his wife by serving, giving way to, and giving himself up for her. Headship and authority modeled on those of Christ does not mean control, giving orders, making unreasonable demands, reducing another human person to the status of servant or, worse, slave to one's every whim. It means service. The Christian husband-head, as Markus Barth puts it so beautifully, becomes "the first servant of his wife."[16] It is such a husband-head, and only such a one, that a wife is to fear (v.33b) as all Christians fear Christ (v.21b).

The reversal of verses 22 and 25 in verse 33 is interesting and significant. Verse 22 enjoined wives to be subject to their husbands and verse 25 enjoined husbands to love their wives. Verse 33 reverses that order, first commanding that husbands love their wives and then warmly wishing that wives fear their husbands. This fear is not fear of a master. Rather it is awe and reverence for loving service, and response to it in a love-as-giving way. Such love cannot be commanded by a tyrant. It is won only by a lover, as the church's love and giving way to Christ is won by a lover who gave, and continues to give, himself for her. This is the author's recipe for becoming one body, joyous giving way in response to, and for the sake of, love. It is a recipe echoed unwittingly by many a modern marriage counselor, though we need to keep in mind that the love the Bible urges upon spouses is not interpersonal affection but loyalty, service, and obedience. That such love is to be mutual is clear from v.21, "Be subject to one another," though it is not stated that a wife is to love her husband. The reasons that the writer adduces for husbands to love their wives apply to all Christians, even to those called wives!

Three reasons are offered to husbands for loving their wives, all of them basically the same. First of all, "husbands should love their wives as [for they are] their own bodies" (v.28a); secondly, the husband "who loves his wife loves himself" (v.28b); thirdly, "the two shall become one body" (v.31b), a reading which is obscured by the Revised Standard Version's "the two shall become one." There is abundant evidence in the Jewish tradition for equating a man's wife to his body.[17] But even if there was no such evidence, the sustained comparison throughout Ephesians 5:21-33 between Christ-Church and husband-wife, coupled with the frequent equation in Ephesians of church and body of Christ (1:22-23; 2:14-16; 3:6; 4:4-16; 5:22-30), clarifies both the meaning of the term *body* and the fact that it is a title of honor rather than of debasement.

Love is always essentially creative. The love of Christ brought into existence the Church and made its believers "members of his body" (v.30). In the same way, the mutual love of a husband and a wife brings such a unity between them that, in image of Christ and Church, she may be called his body and his love for her, therefore, may be called love for his body or for himself. But it is only within the creative love of marriage that, in the Genesis phrase, "the two shall become one body." Prior to marriage, a man did not have this body, nor did a woman have this head. Each receives a gift in marriage, a complement neither had before, which so fulfills each of them that they are no longer two separate persons but one blood person. For each to love the other, therefore, is for each to love herself or himself.

The second reason offered to a husband for loving his wife is that "he who loves his wife loves himself" (v.28b; cp.v.33a). Viewed within the perspective I have just elaborated, such reasoning makes sense. It makes even more Christian sense when one realizes that it is a paraphrase of the great commandment of Leviticus 19:18, cited by Jesus in Mark 12:31: "You shall love your neighbor as yourself." Ephesians, of course, does not say that a husband should love his neighbor as himself, but that he should so love his wife. Where, then, is the link to the great commandment? It is provided through that most beautiful and most sexual of Jewish love songs, the Song of Songs, where in the Septuagint version the lover addresses his bride nine separate times as *plesion*, neighbor (1:9, 15; 2:2,10,13; 4:1,7; 5:2; 6:4). "The context of the occurrence of *plesion* in the Song of Songs confirms that *plesion* is used as a term of endearment for the bride."[18] Other Jewish usage further confirms that conclusion, leaving little doubt that the author of Ephesians had Leviticus 19:18 in mind when instructing a husband to love his wife as himself.

The great Torah and Gospel injunction applies also in marriage: "you shall love your neighbor as yourself." As all Christians are to give way to one another, so also each is to love the other as himself or herself, including husband and wife in marriage. The paraphrase of Leviticus 19:18 repeats in another form what had already been said before in the own-body and the one-body images. What the writer concludes about the Genesis one-body image, namely, "This is a great mystery, and I mean in reference to Christ and the church" (v.32), will conclude our analysis of this central teaching of the New Testament on marriage.

"*This* is a great mystery," namely, as most scholars agree, the Genesis 2:24 text just cited. The mystery, as the Anchor Bible translation seeks to show, is that "this [passage] has an eminent secret meaning," which is that it refers to Christ and the Church. All that has gone before about Christ and the Church comes to the forefront here: that Christ chose the Church to be united to him, as body to head; that he loved the Church and gave himself up for her; that the Church responds to this love of Christ in fear and giving way. Christ who loves the Church, and the Church who responds in love, thus constitute one body, the Body of Christ (Ephesians 1:22-23; 2:14-16; 3:6; 4:4-16; 5:22-30), just as Genesis 2:24 said they would. The writer is well aware that this meaning is not the meaning traditionally given to the text in Judaism, and he states this forthrightly. Just as in the great antithesis of the Sermon on the Mount, Jesus puts forward his interpretations of biblical texts in opposition to traditional interpretations ("You have heard that it was said to the men of old . . . but I say to you"), so also here the writer asserts clearly that it is his own reading of the text ("*I* mean in reference to Christ and the church," v.32 b).

Genesis 2:24 was an excellent text for the purpose the writer had in mind, for it was a central Old Testament text traditionally employed to ordain and legitimate marriage. He acknowledges the meaning that husband and wife become one body in marriage; indeed, in v.33, he returns to and demands that husband and wife live up to this very meaning. But he chooses to go beyond this meaning and insinuate another. Not only does the text refer to the union of husband and wife in marriage, but it refers also to that union of Christ and his church which he has underscored throughout Ephesians 5:1-33. On one level, Genesis 2:24 refers to human marriage; on another level, it refers to the covenant union between Christ and his Church. It is a small step to see human marriage as prophetically representing the covenant between Christ and his Church. In its turn, the union between Christ and his Church provides an ideal model for human marriage and for the mutual conduct of the spouses within it.

Ephesians is not, of course, the only New Testament passage to speak of marriage and of the relationship between husband and wife. Paul does so in 1 Corinthians 7, apparently in response to a question which the Corinthians had submitted to him. The question was: "Is it better for a man to have no relations with a woman?" (7:1). The answer is an implied yes, but not an absolute yes. "Because of the temptation to sexual immorality, each man should have his own wife and each woman her own husband" (7.2). Marriage is good, even for Christians, he seems to say, as a safeguard against sexual sins, a point he underscores again in vv. 5-9. I do not wish to dwell, however, on this unenthusiastic affirmation of marriage. I wish only to highlight the equal relationship Paul assumes in marriage between a husband and a wife, a relationship he makes explicit in vv. 3-4. "The husband should give to the wife her conjugal rights, and likewise the wife to her husband. For the wife does not rule over her own body, but the husband does; likewise the husband does not rule over his own body, but the wife does."

A modern Christian might seize (as did medieval canonists

seeking a precise legal definition of marriage) on Paul's dealing with marital sexual intercourse as an obligation owed mutually by the spouses to one another. But his contemporaries would have seized on something else, something much more surprising to them, namely, his assertion of strict equality between husband and wife in this matter. As Mackin puts it, correctly: "A modern Christian may wince at finding the apostle writing of sexual intercourse as an obligation, or even a debt, owed by spouses to one another, and writing of husbands' and wives' marital relationship as containing authority over one another's bodies. But Paul's contemporaries — at least those bred in the tradition of Torah and of its rabbinic interpreters —would have winced for another reason. This was Paul's assertion of equality between husbands and wives, and equality exactly on the juridical ground of authority and obligations owed."[19]

The author of 1 Timothy 2:8-15 also has something to say about the attitudes of men and women, laying down somewhat disproportionately what is expected of men (v.8) and women (vv.9-15). Of great interest in this text are the two traditional reasons he advances for the authority of men over women and the submission of women to men. The first is that Adam was created before Eve, and the other that it was Eve, not Adam, who was deceived by the serpent. Here the submission of women to men, and therefore of wives to husbands, is legitimated by collected stories of the mythical first human pair. For his part, the author of 1 Peter 3:1-6 requires that wives be submissive to their husbands "as Sarah obeyed Abraham" (v.6). Such widespread views on such Old Testament bases were common in the Jewish world in which the Christian church originated, which makes the attitude of the writer to the Ephesians all the more surprising.

The Old Testament passage that the writer chooses to comment on is one which emphasizes the unity in marriage of the first pair, and therefore of all subsequent pairs, rather than their distinction. He embellishes it not with Old Testament references to creation and to fall, but with New Testament references to the Messiah and to his love. This leads him to a positive appraisal of marriage in the Lord that was not at all customary in the Jewish and Christian milieu of his time. While he echoes the customary *no* to any form of sexual immorality (5:3-5), he offers a more-than-customary *yes* to marriage and sexual intercourse. For him marriage means the union of two people in one body, the formation of a new covenant pair, which is the gift of both God who created it and his Christ who established it in the love he has for the church. So much so that the Christian marriage between a man and a woman becomes the prophetic symbol of the union that exists between Christ and the Church.

This doctrine does not mythicize marriage as an imitation of the marriage of some divine pair, nor does it idealize it so that men and women will not recognize it. Rather it leaves marriage what it is, a secular reality in which a man and a woman seek to become one person in love. What is added is only this, simple and yet mysteriously complex. As they become one body-person in love, they provide through their marriage a prophetic symbol of a similar oneness that exists between their Christ and their Church. Marriage is neither so secular a reality that Christ and Church cannot be represented by it; nor so base a union that it cannot become image and symbol of another, more mysterious union; nor so mythical a reality that women and men cannot live it.

Qualities of Christian Marriage

The qualities of Christian marriage already appear from our biblical analysis. The root quality, the one that irradiates all the others, is the fulfillment of the great Torah and Gospel injunction: "You shall love your neighbor as yourself" (Leviticus 19:18; Mark 12:31; Matthew 19:19). The Apostle Paul instructed the Romans that every other commandment was "summed up in this sentence, 'You shall love your neighbor as yourself' " (13:9). It is an instruction that holds true even, perhaps especially, in marriage. Love, of course, is a reality that is not easy to specify in words. It has a variety of different meanings, and I shall return to them again and again throughout this work. For the moment, I will point out only that in Christian marriage love between the spouses, in fulfillment of the great commandment, is so radically necessary that in our time the Roman Rota, the Supreme Marriage Tribunal of the Roman Catholic Church, has ruled that where it is lacking from the beginning a Christian marriage is invalid.[20] That is how important Christian love is between Christian spouses.

We recall here that covenant love in the Bible is a love that is defined in terms of loyalty, service, and obedience, not in terms of interpersonal affection. The Letter to the Ephesians specifies that the love that is demanded in a Christian marriage is that kind of love. It is, first, love as mutual giving way, love as mutual obedience. The love of the spouses in a Christian marriage is a love that "does not insist on its own way" (1 Corinthians 13:4), a love that does not seek to dominate and control the other spouse. Rather is it a love that seeks to give way to the other whenever possible, so that two persons might become one body. There are individuals whose goal in life appears to be to get their own way always. The New Testament message proclaims that there is no place for such individuals in a marriage, least of all in a Christian marriage. That is not to say that there is no place in a marriage for individual differences. It is to say only that spouses who value getting their own way always, who value the domination of their spouses, who never dream of giving way, will never become one person with anyone, perhaps not even with themselves. In a Christian marriage, love requires not insisting on one's own way, but a mutual empathy with and compassion for the needs, feelings, and desires of one's spouse, and a mutual giving way to those needs, feelings, and desires when the occasion demands for the sake of, and in response to, love. Later, in chapter four, I shall discuss what the Greeks called *eros*, love that seeks its own good, and what they called *agape*, love that seeks the good of another, and I shall indicate how they may be productively allied in a Christian marriage. Here I shall state only that love that is exclusively *eros* is not the kind of love that is apt to ensure that two persons should become one body.

Love in a Christian marriage is, secondly, love as mutual service. All Christians are called to, and are sealed in baptism for, the imitation of Christ, who came "not to be served but to serve" (Mark 10:45). It cannot be otherwise in Christian marriage. In such a marriage there is no master, no mistress, no lady, no lord, but only mutual servants, seeking to be of service to the other, so that each may become one in herself/himself and one also with the other. This is required not just because it is good general counsel for marriage, but specifically because these Christian spouses are called in their marriage both to be imitators of Christ their Lord and to provide a prophetic symbol of his mutual servant-covenant with his church. For Christian spouses their married life is where they are to encounter Christ daily, and thereby come to holiness.

The love that constitutes Christian marriage is, finally, steadfast and faithful. The writer to the Ephesians instructs a husband to love his wife "as Christ loved the church." We can be sure that he intends the same instruction also for a wife. Now Christ loves the Church as Hosea loves Gomer, steadfastly and faithfully. A Christian husband and wife, therefore, are to love each other faithfully. This mutually faithful love, traditionally called fidelity, makes Christian marriage exclusive and permanent, and therefore an indissoluble community of love. I shall have several occasions throughout this book to return to the question of indissolubility. But from the outset I want my position to be clear. Christian marriage is indissoluble because Christian love is steadfast and faithful. Indissolubility is a quality of Christian marriage because it is, first, a quality of Christian love. If marital love exists only inchoately on a wedding day, as it surely does, indissolubility also exists only inchoately. Marital love, as mutual giving way, as mutual service, as mutual fidelity, as mainspring of indissoluble community, is not a given in a Christian marriage but a task to be undertaken. It has an essentially eschatological dimension. *Eschatological* is a grand theological word for a simple and constant human reality, namely the experience of having to admit "already, but not yet." Already mutual love, but not yet steadfast; already mutual service, but not yet without the desire to control; already one body, but not yet one person; already indissoluble in hope and expectation, but not yet in full human reality; already prophetic representation of the covenant union between Christ and his church, but not yet totally adequate representation. For authentic Christian spouses, Christian marriage is always a challenge to which they are called to respond as followers of the Christ who is for them the prophetic symbol of God.

Summary

Four things we have seen in this chapter need to be underscored. First, human marriage is not an imitation of the eternal marriage of some divine couple, but a truly human, and therefore truly secular, reality which man and woman, *'adam*, hold as their own as gift from their Creator-God. In the giving and receiving of this gift, the Giver, the gift and the recipient are essentially and forever bound together. Secondly, this bond is explicated by the prophet Hosea, who brings into conscious focus the fact that marriage between a man and a woman is also the prophetic symbol of the covenant union between Yahweh and his people. Thirdly, the author of the letter to the Ephesians further clarifies the symbolic nature of marriage by proclaiming "a great mystery." The great mystery is that as a man and a woman become one body-person in marriage, so also are Christ and his Church one body-person, and that the one reflects the other. From such thinking Roman Catholic theologians will be led slowly to declare that *human* marriage, on occasion, may be also *Christian* sacrament. Fourthly, Christian marriage is both a covenant and a community of love between a man and a woman, love that does not seek its own, love that gives way, love that serves, love that is steadfastly faithful. Because it is a covenant and a community of steadfast love, it is a permanent and exclusive state and a prophetic symbol of the steadfast covenant and community of love between Christ and his Church. That Christian marriage is such a reality, though, is not something that is to be taken blindly as being so. Rather it is something that in steadfast continuity is to be made so. Permanence is not a static, ontological quality of a marriage, but a dynamic, living quality of human love on which marriage, both human and Christian, thrives.

Questions for Reflection and Discussion

1. In your judgment, what is the radical distinction between the ancient Jewish mythology about sexuality, marriage, and fertility and that of the peoples surrounding them in the ancient Near East? Does that distinction make any contribution to the mythology you hold about those same realities?

2. If you believed that sexuality and marriage were gifts of God, would that be enough for you to say that they related you to God? If you believed they were gifts of God, would that be enough for you to say that they were sacramental? If yes, in what sense?

3. Do you look upon marriage as sacramental? What does *sacramental* mean to you?

4. The two great commandments in Judaism and Christianity prescribe

the love of God and the love of neighbor. According to the letter to the Ephesians, how are these commandments to be lived in a Christian marriage?

5. What does it mean to you to say that a man and a woman become one body in marriage? Do you understand their one-body relationship to be a legal or a kind of blood relationship? If it were a kind of blood relationship, how would you go about getting a divorce?

From Bible to Church: Developing Doctrine About Marriage

What was said about marriage in the opening chapter was said out of a predominantly Jewish context. The developing Christian church soon moved out of that Jewish context into a Greco-Roman one in which Fathers of the Church developed their doctrine about marriage.

The Teaching of the Greek Fathers

We must keep in mind two things as we begin to consider their teaching. First, the Fathers reflect their times in their writings. We ought not to be surprised, then, when we find them saying things about men, women, and marriage that we would not say in our time. We ought not be surprised, for instance, when they assume that marriage is a union between two persons of quite unequal social value, a man who chooses a wife and a woman for whom her father chooses a husband. The early and anonymous *Epistle to Diognetus* portrays the general situation of these and all early Christians. "Neither in region nor in tongue nor in the social institutions of life do Christians differ from other men. . . . They take wives as all do, and they procreate children, but they do not abort the fetus."[1] Secondly, because the teaching of the early Fathers on marriage was almost exclusively a defense of marriage against certain errors which threatened both its Christian value and its future, we find no systematic and full treatment of marriage as a social and Christian institution. The majority of these errors had Gnostic sources, and it will be to our benefit to consider, however briefly, the Gnosticism from which they came.

Gnosticism, a religious philosophy characterized by the doctrine that salvation is achieved through a special knowledge (*gnosis*), antedated Christianity and exercised a great influence on many Christian communities in the Mediterranean basin. Christian Gnostics came to look upon themselves as the only faithful interpreters of the Jesus movement. They disagreed with orthodox Christian teaching on two major points: first, they preached predestination, denying any free will in either salvation or damnation; secondly, they preached a very dualistic and pessimistic view of the world, a view in which good and evil are equally real. Both of these views affected their attitude toward marriage, and therefore the Fathers' expositions on marriage in reaction.

The most completely elaborated Gnostic teaching on predestination was perhaps that of the Roman Gnostic Valentinus. He taught that people are composed of three quite separate elements, matter (*hyle*), soul (*psyche*), and spirit (*pneuma*). Depending on which of these elements dominates in any given person, there results three quite different kinds, hylics, psychics, and spiritual people or pneumatics. Hylics, he taught, are predestined to damnation and are quite unredeemable: they constitute the majority of humanity. Pneumatics are predestined to salvation; they constitute a small minority of humanity, the true Gnostics. Psychics are evil, because soul is evil, but they can be saved by their free decision to participate in the *gnosis* of the Gnostics. Pneumatics, being spiritual and saved,

are beyond anything that is material, and therefore disdain marriage
and look upon it as evil.

Because matter was essentially evil, they believed, it could not
have been created by a good God. That meant that Gnostics had to
revise the classic Jewish-Christian approach to creation. That task
was accomplished by Marcion, the son of the bishop of Sinope. He
taught that, of necessity, there had to be two gods, one a creator god
who is the source of evil, the other the supreme god who is the source
of goodness and salvation. The god who created evil is Yahweh, the
god of the Old Testament; the supreme god is the Father of Jesus,
who alone reveals him. The Old Testament, which reveals the evil
deity, was created by hylics who have long since gone to their predestined damnation. It should be rejected, therefore, by the pneumatics,
along with all its doctrines and its laws. Among such doctrines is the
doctrine that men, women, and marriage were created good by God.
Among such laws are those that legislate the relationships of men and
women and their mutual sexual activity. Pneumatic Gnostics have
risen above such laws and have no need to follow them. It is easy to
see how such attitudes could generate, on the one hand, a negative
ascetic approach to sexuality and marriage and, on the other hand, a
licentious, permissive approach (which was known as antinomian-
ism). The second and third century Fathers had to defend marriage
against attacks on both these fronts.

By the middle of the second century of the Christian era,
Alexandria had become established as the intellectual capital of the
Hellenistic world. We would expect to find powerful Gnostics there,
and that our expectation is not false is verified in the writings of the
bishop of Alexandria, Clement. He tells us that there are the two
kinds of Gnostics we have noted, namely, the kind who abstain from
marriage and sexual intercourse because they believe them to be evil,
and the antinomians who believe they are saved no matter what and
are, therefore, above any law regarding sexuality and marriage.[2] He
tells us of the ascetic Julius Cassianus whose work *On Continence* he
cites. "Let no one say that because we have these members, that
because the female is structured this way and the male that way, the
one to give the seed and the other to receive it, that the custom of
sexual intercourse is allowed by God. For if this structure were from
God, toward whom we tend, he would not have pronounced blessed
those who are eunuchs. And the prophet would not have said that

they 'are not an unfruitful tree' (Isaiah 56:3), transferring from the tree to the man who by his own will castrates himself of such thought."[3]

Clement declares such an opinion "impious." His response is a simple one: marriage was created by the one true God and, therefore, was good from its origin. "If marriage according to the law is sinful," he argues, "I do not see how anyone can say he knows God, and say that sin was commanded by God. But if the law is holy, marriage is holy. The apostle, therefore, refers this mystery to Christ and the church."[4] Irenaeus of Lyons employs this same argument in his extensive refutation of the Gnostics. He mentions Marcion and Saturninus, "who are called the continent," and accuses them of frustrating the ancient plan of God and of finding fault with him "who made both male and female for the begetting of men."[5]

Those who attack sexuality and marriage as evil, Clement argues, attack the will of God and the mystery of creation, to which even the Virgin and Jesus were subject.[6] Marriage is primarily for procreation,[7] "for the sake of the race, the succession of children and, as far as is in us, the perfection of the world."[8] It is for something else, too, quite predictable in the culture of the time, namely, for a wife to bring help to her husband in the running of his household,[9] particularly in his sickness and old age.[10] It is finally a union in which "a pious wife seeks to persuade her husband, if she can, to be a companion to her in those things that lead to salvation."[11]

If the reply to the ascetic Gnostics was with an argument external to the nature of marriage, namely, marriage is good because it was created by God, the reply to the antinomians was based on what was taken to be the very nature of sexuality and, therefore, marriage. The antinomian posture may be exemplified in the teachings of Carpocrates, against whom both Clement and Irenaeus contend. He teaches that Jesus, the Son of Joseph, escaped from the control of the creators of the world by a power he received from his father, the supreme God. After Jesus, those men who can attain the same power by knowledge and magic can make the same escape. Since they have freed themselves from the powers of this world, and since they are predestined to salvation, they are freed also from the moral laws of this world and can engage in any kind of conduct without danger. Both Clement and Irenaeus accuse them of engaging in sexual immoralities, even in connection with the great *agape* meal.[12] They counter the antinomian position with an appeal to the nature of sexuality as understood from sexual structure.

The early Christian understanding of the nature of sexuality resembles that of the Stoics. It is most precisely represented in a statement from the Christian African, Lactantius. "Just as God gave us eyes, not that we might look upon and desire pleasure, but that we might see those actions that pertain to the necessity of life, so also we have received the genital part of the body for no other purpose than the begetting of offspring, as the very name itself teaches. This divine law is to be obeyed with the greatest of devotion."[13] This was a commonly accepted teaching, which carried with it several conclusions: first, that by its very nature sexual intercourse was for the procreation of children; secondly, any such intercourse for purposes other than procreation was a violation of nature; and thirdly, any sexual intercourse when conception is impossible is a similar violation. From this established position Christian Fathers would argue that Gnostics, or anyone else, engaging in sexual intercourse for any purpose other than procreation were in violation of nature. It is an argument that some Church Fathers continue to offer in the twentieth century.

Already in the second century, in his apology for Christians, Justin Martyr had replied to Roman accusations about the sexual immorality of Christians by insisting that "either we marry only to have children or, if we do not marry, we are continent always."[14] But Clement goes much further, arguing that the only purpose for sexual intercourse is to beget a child and that any other purpose must be excluded. "A man who marries for the procreation of children," he argues, "must exercise continence, lest he desire his wife whom he ought to love, and so that he may beget children with chaste and moderated will. For we are not children of desire but of will."[15] Origen, his fellow Alexandrian, is just as clear, arguing that the man who has sexual intercourse only with his wife, "and with her only at certain legitimate times and only for the sake of children," is truly circumcised.[16] He underscores what he means by legitimate times, insisting that once a wife has conceived, intercourse is no longer good. Those who indulge in sexual intercourse with their own wives after they are already pregnant are worse than beasts, "for even beasts know that, once they have conceived, they do not indulge their mates with their largesse."[17]

The third century Syrian *Didascalia Apostolorum*, a collection of disciplinary laws, also declares intercourse during pregnancy as immoral, and situates the immorality in the fact that such intercourse is "not for the begetting of children, but for the sake of pleasure. Now a lover of God ought not to be a lover of pleasure."[18] In the Latin West, that judgment was taken so much for granted that Ambrose of Milan would explain that Saint Elizabeth was embarrassed at conceiving a child in her old age, because she knew that those who are barren violate nature when they engage in sexual intercourse. Since they have no hope of conceiving a child, "which is the sole reason for intercourse," their intercourse must be sparked by desire, which is immoral.[19] Another Latin, Jerome, always blunt, declares that intercourse is to be named lust and uncleanness if it is not moderated and under the eyes of God.[20] Long before Clement, Origen, Ambrose, and Jerome, Musonius Rufus, the great Stoic, had advanced the same position. "Men who are not wantons or immoral are bound to consider sexual intercourse justified only when it occurs in marriage and is indulged in for the purpose of begetting children, since that is lawful, but unjust and unlawful when it is mere pleasure-seeking, even in marriage."[21] The fact that Origen, in his apology for Christianity, named Musonius and Socrates as examples of the highest kind of life, as the two great pagan saints, so to speak, might be a very good indication of the pagan origins of such teaching.[22]

The Teaching of the Latin Fathers

Two great Fathers of the Western church advanced the church's thinking on marriage and left it with a theology of marriage that became a given in Christian thinking for centuries afterwards. The lesser one is Tertullian who wrote about marriage in both the orthodox Catholic and heretical Montanist periods of his life. In his first book, *To A Wife*, he exhibits the same ambivalence to sexuality and marriage that we have seen already in Origen. He grants that in the beginning marriage was necessary to populate the earth, but argues that when the end of the world is near there is no need for such activity. Paul may have *allowed* marriage as an antidote to desire, but Tertullian is in no doubt: "how much better it is neither to marry nor to burn (with concupiscence)." He will not even allow that marriage can be called good, for "what is *allowed* is not good . . . nor is anything good just because it is not evil."[23]

One would be excused for thinking that Tertullian has no time for marriage. But this same man, who is so pessimistic about marriage in his first book, in a second book with the same title writes the most beautiful lines on Christian marriage that one could ever hope to find.

> How can we suffice to tell the joy of that marriage which the church consecrates. . . . What a bond is that of two faithful who are of one hope, one discipline, one service; both are brothers, both are servants. There is no separation of spirit and flesh. They are truly two in one flesh, and where there is one flesh there is also one spirit. They pray together, they sleep together, they fast together, teaching one another, exhorting one another, sustaining one another.[24]

One might conclude, with some legitimacy, that between the first and second books Tertullian had found a wonderful wife. When he became a Montanist, however, he regressed to his earlier judgment that Paul had simply allowed marriage which is, though not a sin, none the less a blot on a perfect Christian life.[25]

When we reach Augustine, the Bishop of Hippo, we reach the systematic insight into the nature of marriage that was to mold and control the doctrine of the Western church down to our own day, so much so that Augustine is sometimes called the doctor of Christian marriage. His influence is always felt in talk about marriage. Pius XI, for instance, in the opening of his influential encyclical on Christian marriage, *Casti Connubii,* turned to him as to the wellspring of the truths about Christian marriage to which the Catholic Church adheres. Vatican Council II also turned to him, developing its teaching about marriage within the schema of the threefold good of marriage as he described it.[26] Although the influence of Augustine's teaching on marriage cannot be doubted, there are many who feel that the influence has not been always positive. We must, therefore, look closely at his teaching on marriage. That teaching must be viewed in its context, a context which is again a defense against attack. As the Alexandrians defended sexuality and marriage against the attacks of the Gnostics, so did Augustine defend them against the attacks of the Manichees and Pelagians. We need to say a word, therefore, about these two.

The Manichees took their name from their founder, Mani, born in Babylonia about the year 216. Mani claimed to have received from an angel, at ages twelve and twenty-four, the definitive revelation about the nature of the world and of history. Here we need consider only those aspects of Manicheeism which impinge on its teaching about marriage. First, it is a dualistic system, the dual opposites being good and evil, light and darkness, spirit and matter. Sexuality is listed among the dark and evil realities, along with wine and meat. Secondly, since Mani was looked upon as the ultimate prophet in the line of Jesus, he was said to have completed the latter's teachings and to have organized the ultimate church. That church had two kinds of members, a group of the perfect and a group of auditors, those we would call today catechumens. The perfect always abstained from wine, meat, and sexual activity; the auditors abstained only on Sundays. It is not too difficult to guess what was the Manichean approach to sexuality and marriage. Both were evil in themselves and, therefore, to be avoided. Against this approach Augustine will repeat the argument of Clement and Irenaeus. Sexuality and marriage, created by God, must be essentially good.

Pelagianism derived its name from a Briton, Pelagius, who lived in Rome around the year 380. The Pelagian attack against Augustine, though, was led more by a disciple of Pelagius, Julian, Bishop of Eclanum, than by Pelagius himself. The argument between Augustine and the Pelagians centered around the extent of our original fall from grace. Augustine taught that the original sin had seriously impaired human nature, so that after the Fall men and women could not do without grace what they had been able to do without it before the Fall. The Pelagians, on the other hand, taught that the Fall had left human nature unimpaired, so that men and women could do after the Fall exactly what they had been capable of doing prior to the Fall without any help from grace. Against the Pelagians Augustine will teach that the results of the Fall, encapsulated in what he called *concupiscence*, make it very difficult to avoid sin in sexual intercourse, even in marriage. Pelagians, therefore, will accuse him of being a Manichee and of teaching that marriage and sexual intercourse are necessarily evil. They will be followed in this by many a modern writer who adverts only to Augustine's anti-Pelagian writings.[27] For such a complex writer, caught in the crossfire of two quite opposing heresies, we can guess that it is too simple a procedure to be correct.

Augustine's basic statement about sexuality and marriage is ubiquitous, firm, and clear. Contrary to those Manichee heretics who hold that sexuality is evil and who condemn and prohibit marriage and sexual intercourse,[28] he states that sexuality and marriage were created good by God and cannot lose that God-gifted intrinsic goodness.[29] He specifies the good of marriage as threefold and insists that even after the Fall the marriages of many devout Christians still contain this threefold good: fidelity, offspring, sacrament. "It is expected that in fidelity neither partner will indulge in sexual activity outside of marriage; that offspring will be lovingly accepted, kindly nurtured, and religiously educated; that in sacrament the marriage will not be dissolved and that neither partner will be dismissed to marry another, not even for the sake of offspring."[30] In this triple good Augustine intends the mutual fidelity of the spouses, the procreation and education of the children, and the indissolubility of the marriage. Among these three he generally gives priority to procreation, because "from this derives the propagation of the human race in which a loving community is a great good."[31] And yet, to some extent at least, the good of sacrament is valued above the good of procreation, for he insists, as we have just seen, that a marriage cannot be dissolved, "not even for the sake of offspring." There may be here the seed of a Christian attitude to marriage that moves away from the *social* priority of procreation to the *interpersonal* priority of loving community between the spouses, in the image of the loving community between Christ and the Church. We shall see later that these two priorities have been given quite different weights at different times in Roman Catholic history, and that in the contemporary Roman Catholic approach they are given equal weights.

There is in Augustine, alongside the tradition of the threefold good of marriage, another tradition of another good, that of friendship between the sexes. In *The Good of Marriage,* after asserting that marriage is good and that there is merit in asking why it is good, he gives an interesting answer. "It does not seem to me to be good only because of the procreation of children, but also because of the natural companionship between the sexes. Otherwise, we could not speak of marriage in the case of old people, especially if they had either lost their children or had begotten none at all"[32] Later in the same work he returns to that idea. "God gives us some goods which are to be sought for their own sake, such as wisdom, health, friendship; others which are necessary for something else, such as learning, food, drink, marriage, sexual intercourse. Certain of these are necessary for the sake of wisdom, such as learning; others for the sake of health, such as food and drink and sleep; others *for the sake of friendship, such as marriage or intercourse,* for from this comes the propagation of the human race in which friendly association is a great good."[33] There is one further text in this tradition which ought to be cited. "A Christian man can live at peace with his wife. He can supply with her, either for the need of the flesh which the Apostle (Paul) gives as a permission, not as a command; or for the propagation of children, which is praiseworthy on a certain level; or for companionship, having her as a sister without any mingling of bodies, which in the marriage of Christians is most excellent and sublime."[34]

"In these passages," as Mackin says, "Augustine has enriched the source whence Catholic canonists and theologians will later draw one of their 'secondary ends' of marriage, that one whose name least exactly describes its nature because the name can refer to so much —the *mutuum adiutorium* of the spouses, their mutual help, or support."[35] I believe he has done more. He has falsified in advance the claim of those who say that only in modern times has sexual intercourse and marriage been seen in relation to the relationship and love of spouses.[36] But the source of what appears problematic in Augustine's teaching about marriage seems always to derive from what he says against the Pelagians. To this, therefore, we must now turn.

The basic position can be stated quite unequivocally, and there can be no doubt about it. Sexual intercourse between a husband and a wife, in Augustine's judgment, is created good. It can, however, as can any good, be used sinfully. In the latter case, though, it is not the good itself which is sinful, but its disordered use. It is a balanced principle to which he will return at the end of his life in his *Retractationes.* Evil and sin are never substantial, but are only in the will; there is, nevertheless, in men and women a concupiscence that causes sin.[37] With the basic position in mind, it is not difficult to understand all that Augustine says about sexualty and marriage. Against the Pelagian, Julian, he explains carefully: "Evil does not follow because marriages are good, but because in the good things of marriage there is also a use that is evil. Sexual intercourse was not created because of the concupiscence of the flesh, but because of good. That good would have remained without that evil if no one had sinned."[38] It is clear that he is saying that there is one thing that is good, namely, sexual intercourse, and another thing that is evil, namely, concupiscence, that can translate that good into evil. His position is much more nuanced than many notice: sexual intercourse is good in itself, but there are conditions under which it is good and conditions under which it is evil.

The condition under which it is good is the classic Stoic condition we have already seen in the Alexandrians, when it is for the begetting of a child. Any other use, even between the spouses in marriage, is at least venially sinful. "Conjugal sexual intercourse for the sake of offspring is not sinful. But sexual intercourse, even with one's spouse, to satisfy concupiscence is a venial sin. Adultery or fornication, however, is a mortal sin."[39] It is not sexual intercourse between spouses that is sinful, but only such intercourse controlled by concupiscence. Marital intercourse for the Stoically natural reason, the procreation of children, is good. Intercourse as a result of concupiscence is sinful. By concupiscence he means the disordered pursuit by any appetite of its proper good, a pursuit which since the Fall is difficult to keep within the proper, reasonable limits. In effect, since the fall of humanity and the rise of concupiscence, the sexual appetite is always threatened by concupiscence and, therefore, by sinfulness. It is not, though, the sexual appetite that is sinful; that is good. The Fathers of the Old Testament, he argues, took a "natural delight" in sexual intercourse and it was not sinful because it "was in no way given rein up to the point of unreasoning and wicked desire."[40] It is clear that it is disordered and unreasonable sexual desire and intercourse fired by concupiscence that is sinful, not sexual desire or intercourse *per se*. "Whatever, therefore, spouses do together that is immodest, shameful, filthy, is the vice of men, not the fault of marriage."[41]

Pope Gregory the Great shared Augustine's judgment that, because of the presence of concupiscence, even that genital pleasure between spouses in the act of procreation is sinful. He went further and banned from access to the church those who had just had pleasurable intercourse. "The custom of the Romans from antiquity," he explained, "has always been, after sexual intercourse with one's spouse, both to cleanse oneself by washing and to abstain reverently from entering the church for a time. In saying this we do not intend to say that sexual intercourse is sinful. But because every lawful sexual intercourse between spouses cannot take place without bodily pleasure, they are to refrain from entering the holy place. For such pleasure cannot be without sin."[42] It is not difficult to see how such a doctrine could produce a strong ambivalence towards sexuality and marriage. That ambivalence weighed heavily in subsequent history on the theory and practice of Christian marriage. It weighed just as heavily on the theory and practice of Christian celibacy, for as Schillebeeckx notes, "even the relatively recent law of celibacy is governed by the antiquated and ancient conviction that there is something unclean and slightly sinful about sexual intercourse (even in the context of sacramental marriage)."[43] That antiquated and ancient conviction gave rise to another conviction in the Western church, namely, the conviction that virginity and celibacy are superior to marriage and that those who are celibate are holier, and therefore, superior to those who are married.

The Scholastic Doctrine

Augustine's teaching controlled the approach to marriage in the Western Church until the thirteenth century. The high Scholastics then made some significant alterations and additions to it. Thomas Aquinas took over Augustine's three *goods* of marriage and transformed them into the three *ends* of marriage. This change in terminology was dictated by his view of humanity. Thomas shared with Aristotle the view that people, though sharing in the genus animal, were constituted a species apart from all other animals by their reason. This reason enables them to apprehend the ends proper to *human* animals, inscribed in the so-called natural law flowing from the design of the creator God. And so, what were for Neo-Platonic Augustine *goods* of marriage become for Aristotelian Aquinas *ends* of marriage, and ends established in a "natural" priority.

> Marriage has as its principal end the procreation and education of offspring, an end which belongs to man by reason of his generic nature and which, therefore, is shared with other animals. And so offspring are said to be a good of marriage. But, as the Philosopher [Aristotle] says, it has a secondary end in man alone, the sharing of tasks which are necessary in life, and from this point of view husband and wife owe each other faithfulness, which is one of the goods of marriage. There is yet

another end in believers, namely, the meaning of Christ and church, and so a good of marriage is called sacrament. The first end is found in marriage in so far as man is animal, the second in so far as he is man, the third in so far as he is believer.[44]

As is customary in Aquinas, this is a tight and sharply delineated argument, and its terminology *primary end–secondary end* came to dominate discussion of the ends of marriage in Roman Catholic manuals for seven hundred years. But neither the sharpness of the argument nor the undoubted authority of the author should be allowed to obscure the fact that it is also a very curious argument, for it makes the claim that the primary end of specifically *human* marriage is dictated by a man's generically *animal* nature. I intend to challenge this claim later.

Thomas, of course, wishes to insist always that reason must have control. Not that there is any rational control *in* the act of sexual intercourse, for "animals lack reason. Therefore, in sexual intercourse man becomes an animal, for the pleasure of the action and the force of the desire cannot be moderated by reason."[45] But there is reason *before* intercourse, and because there is, sexual intercourse between a husband and a wife is not sinful. The excess of passion which corrupts virtue (and which is, therefore, as in Augustine, sinful) is that which not only impedes reason, but also destroys it. Such is not the case with the intensity of pleasure in sexual intercourse for, "though a man is not then under control, he has been under the control of reason in advance."[46] Besides, nature has been created good by God, so that "it is impossible to say that the act in which offspring are created is so completely unlawful that the means of virtue cannot be found in it."[47]

There remains some ambivalence towards sexual desire, activity and pleasure. They are "occupations with lower affairs which distract the soul and make it unworthy of being joined actually to God."[48] But they are not sinful at all times and in all circumstances. Indeed, within the ends of marriage they are meritorious,[49] and Thomas asserts explicitly that to forego the pleasure and thwart the end would be sinful.[50] This latter opinion leads Messenger to go beyond Aquinas and declare that "both passion and pleasure are natural concomitants of the sex act, and so far from diminishing its goodness, if the sex act is willed beforehand according to right reason, the effect of pleasure and passion is simply to heighten and increase the moral goodness of the act, not in any way to diminish it."[51] That is an interesting opinion, quite defensible within Aquinas's system and quite in line, too, with Augustine's judgment about the "natural delight" taken in sexual intercourse by the Fathers of the Old Testament. It is also a far cry from Gregory, and a move toward both the liberation of marriage and legitimate sexual intercourse from any taint of sin and their recognition as a sign and a cause of grace, that is, as a sacrament.

The early Scholastics did not doubt that marriage was a sign of grace, but they did doubt that it was a cause of grace. They hesitated, therefore, to include it among the sacraments of the church. Peter Lombard, for instance, defined sacrament in the categories of sign and cause. "A sacrament, properly speaking, is a sign of the grace of God and the form of invisible grace in such a way that it is its image and its cause. Sacraments are instituted, therefore, not only for signifying grace but also for causing it."[52] He proceeds to list the sacraments of the New Law, carefully distinguishing marriage from sacraments properly so called. "Some offer a remedy for sin and confer helping grace, such as baptism; others offer a remedy only, such as marriage; others support us with grace and virtue, such as eucharist and orders."[53] Marriage is a sacrament for Lombard only in the very general sense that it is a sign, "a sacred sign of a sacred reality, namely, the union of Christ and the church."[54]

It was the Dominicans, Albert the Great and Thomas Aquinas, who firmly established marriage among the sacraments of the church. In his commentary on Lombard, Albert lists the various opinions about the sacramentality of marriage and characterizes as "very probable" the opinion which holds that "it confers grace for doing good, not just any good but that good specifically that a married person should do."[55] In his commentary on the same Lombard, Aquinas goes further, characterizing as "most probable" the opinion that "marriage, in so far as it is contracted in faith in Christ, confers grace to do those things which are required in marriage."[56] In his *Contra Gentiles* he is even more positive, stating bluntly that "it is to be believed that through this sacrament [marriage] grace is given to the married."[57] By the time he wrote his completed thought in the *Summa Theologiae*, he lists marriage among the seven sacraments with no demur whatever about its grace-conferring qualities. The combined theological authority of Albert and Thomas ensured for marriage, albeit late in Christian history, a place among the sacraments of the Roman Catholic Church. By the time of the Reformation their opinion was held universally by theologians.

The Teaching of the Church

In the Middle Ages, under the banners of the Cathari and Albigenses, the Neo-Platonic and Gnostic dualism which the Fathers combated but never definitively put to rest enjoyed a period of resurgence. There was again a widespread suspicion and downright negative pessimism toward sexuality and marriage, and once again the church intervened to defend these good gifts of God. The second Lateran Council (1139) condemned those who "condemn the bonds of legitimate marriage," and ordered them "to be coerced by external powers"[58] to accept the goodness and legitimacy of marriage. While talk of external coercion might make us wince today, we can still be glad of the convincing evidence it offers of how strongly the church felt about the goodness of legitimate sexuality and marriage. Catharism was castigated further in the Council of Verona (1184) where, for the first time in a document of the church, marriage was listed as a sacrament in the company of baptism, eucharist, and confession.[59] As part of the formula for healing the great schism between East and West, the Council of Lyons (1274) listed marriage among seven sacraments,[60] a listing repeated by the Council of Florence (1439), with the specification that these seven sacraments "both contain grace and confer it on those who receive them worthily."[61]

The concluding section of the Florentine decree deals explicitly with marriage, and is an excellent summary of everything that had been taught about it until then. "'The seventh sacrament is marriage, which is a sign of the union between Christ and his church. . . . A triple good [not *end*] is designated for marriage. The first is offspring accepted and raised to worship God; the second is fidelity, in which each spouse ought to serve the other; the third is the indivisibility of marriage because it signifies the indivisible union of Christ and Church. And, although separation is permissible in the case of fornication [*sic*], remarriage is not, for the bond of legitimately contracted marriage is perpetual."[62] That marriage is a sacrament, that it contains and confers grace, that it is indissoluble, all these are now established doctrines in the Western Church. When the Council of Trent teaches them in response to the Reformers, it is not inventing, but merely stating, the established doctrine and faith of the church.[63] I see no need to go over that ground again. There is one decision Trent made about marriage, though, that I must reflect on, because in its time it was an important and innovative response to a pressing problem. I refer to the decree *Tametsi,* which sought to eliminate clandestine marriages by establishing a legal form without which marriage is not valid.

In a community of believers who hold that marriage is a sacrament, that it symbolizes the union of Christ and his Church, confers grace on those who receive it worthily, and is indissoluble, a crucial question needs to be settled. It is an apparently simple, but in reality a very complex, question: when is there a sacramental marriage? At what precise moment in time are two persons sacramentally and indissolubly married? This question vexed Western Church lawyers and, to a lesser extent, theologians for centuries, for in the Western tradition it had two quite differing answers.

There was the Roman answer: consent between a man and a woman makes marriage. There was the northern European answer: sexual intercourse between a man and a woman after the giving of consent makes marriage. Both answers, of course, had long cultural histories, each with good reasons why it should be so. When the Church, then, came to formulate an answer to the question of what really makes an indissoluble marriage, there were proponents of both sides. I do not intend to detail the resulting discussions, since for the purposes of this book they have only tangential interest.[64] All I need to do here is outline what came to be the final solution.

By the middle of the twelfth century the lines of the consent or intercourse debate had taken clear shape, the theologians of the University of Paris championing the Roman tradition, and the canonists of the University of Bologna the European. The Master at Bologna in the mid-twelfth century was Gratian, who around 1140 completed a work of collecting and harmonizing all the texts of marriage available to him at the time. The work, usually known simply as *Gratian's Decree,* sought to offer a solution to the problem of consent or intercourse by combining the two, employing a distinction already introduced by his Parisian opponents.

That distinction was between *matrimonium initiatum* (initiated marriage) and *matrimonium ratum* (completed marriage), and Gratian employed it to harmonize the two divergent opinions. Consent makes an initiated marriage; subsequent sexual intercourse makes a ratified and consummated marriage. "It should be known that marriage is initiated by betrothal (consent), perfected by sexual intercourse. Therefore, between spouses there is marriage, but only initiated; between spouses who have engaged in sexual intercourse, there is ratified marriage."[65] This compromise opinion ultimately passed into the law of the Roman Church, and was enshrined in its *Code of Canon Law* in the twentieth century as a distinction between *matrimonium ratum,* that is, marriage ratified by the church, and *matrimonium ratum et consummatum,* that is, marriage ratified by the church and completed by the spouses in their sexual intercourse.[66]

To contemporary lovers such intricacies probably appear as so much indelicate nit-picking. "We love one another" seems to them a sufficient answer to almost any question. But history shows that at the time it was more than just nit-picking. There was, to cite just one example, a classic marriage dispute and an influential decision rendered in the ninth century by Hincmar, Bishop of Rheims. The dispute involved Stephen, a noble of Aquitaine, and the daughter of another Aquitaine noble, Regimund. Stephen exchanged marriage consent with the lady but refused to consummate the marriage, and on that basis claimed freedom from it. Hincmar, following the Frankish tradition, ruled in favor of Stephen, albeit a trifle ambiguously. He argued that consummation is essential for creating a marriage and that there is no real marriage without it, basing his judgment on the argument that without intercourse the couple has not yet tried to realize the prime good of marriage, namely, offspring. "Let it be known that betrothal, dowry and nuptials, such as took place here, are not a marriage, since the union of the sexes was lacking and, on that account, both the hope of offspring and the sacrament of faith."[67] Gratian would have approved of Hincmar's judgment, for with his distinction between *matrimonium initiatum* and *matrimonium ratum* he would have ruled in the same way.

Another consideration that shows that all of this was not just medieval nit-picking is the history of clandestine marriages. A clandestine marriage is one that is contracted by the simple exchange of consent between a man and a woman without any publicity or any witnesses. By the late Middle Ages such marriages had become a scourge in Europe. They took place between couples who could not marry publicly because their parents would not allow it or a class distinction forbade it or any one of countless other reasons. Unfortunately, after a time, many such marriages came to a litigated end, with charge and countercharge of concubinage, fornication, and illegitimacy.

The Roman opinion acknowledged the validity of such marriages, for consent makes marriage; the European opinion acknowledged the validity of such marriages when they were consummated; after Gratian, the Roman Church acknowledged the indissolubility of such consummated marriages. That such indissoluble marriages, sacraments of the unending union between Christ and the Church, would simply cease to be at someone's unsubstantiated whim was intolerable for the Church. Already in the ninth century, the Eastern church had tried to put an end to clandestine marriages, the Emperor Leo IV decreeing that any attempt to marry without ecclesiastical witnesses rendered the marriage null. In the sixteenth century the Council of Trent also tried to proscribe them, decreeing in *Tametsi* that a true and valid marriage, one that the Church would recognize as sacramental and indissoluble, must be celebrated publicly in the presence of a duly appointed priest and two witnesses.[68] Only if celebrated in this form, as it came to be called, would a marriage be recognized as valid.

Tametsi transformed marriage from a simple contract, one not restricted by any external legal requirements, to a solemn contract, one in which certain legal formalities had to be met for the contract to be valid. That transformation required a parallel transformation in the form in which the sacrament of marriage was celebrated, but that change was only in the externals of the celebration and not in the substance of the sacrament. After *Tametsi*, as before, the sacrament of marriage is still constituted by the consent of the man and the woman, and the marriage is constituted indissoluble by their subsequent intercourse. The change introduced by Trent's decree was well within the powers of the Church to make, and it is similarly within its power to make any analogous change today in the externalization of the man's and woman's giving of consent. I shall return to this point later.

Summary

I wish to underscore three points from this chapter. First, a very negative attitude toward sexuality and its use in marriage crept into Christianity from heretical Gnostic and Stoic sources. Though this attitude was combated consistently by theologians and church councils, it remains still rooted in the ongoing Christian ethos about marriage. Secondly, this negative attitude toward sexuality contributed to the enthronement, however implicit, of several judgments in the Catholic tradition. Among these are: marriage, involving sexuality and therefore somehow evil, cannot be a cause of grace, that is, cannot be a sacrament; virginity and celibacy are superior, and therefore preferable, to marriage; Holy Orders and those in Holy Orders are holier, and therefore superior, to marriage and those in marriage. These judgments have left their mark on the Roman Catholic tradition; they are quite nonsensical when measured against the biblical tradition elaborated in our first chapter. Finally, with the acceptance of Christian marriage as a sacrament, came the need to specify just when a sacramental marriage took place and was indissoluble. Gratian's distinction between initiated marriage, which is fully valid but dissoluble marriage, and consummated marriage, which is a fully valid and indissoluble marriage, contributed an important response to that need. Trent's *Tametsi*, which decreed an entirely novel form without which Christians could enter neither a valid marriage nor a valid sacrament, contributed another. Gratian's distinction and Trent's form became inscribed in the Canon Law of the Roman Church, and still control answers to questions which arise about not only the legality and validity of marriage, but also about its sacramentality. I shall challenge some of these questions and answers in the following chapters.

Questions for Reflection and Discussion

1. In your opinion, does the negative attitude toward sexuality inherited from Stoicism, Gnosticism, and Manicheeism persist in contemporary Christianity? How does it manifest itself?

2. How is that negative attitude to be reconciled with the biblical

information that sexuality is a creation of the good God and, therefore, good?

3. What exactly does the word *procreation* mean to you? Does it make any difference whether procreation is said to be a good or an end of marriage? What difference is there?

4. Is it any way meaningful to you that the physical consummation of a marriage plays such an important role in determining the completeness, and therefore the indissolubility, of a marriage? Do you see any reason to suggest that personal consummation is much more important than physical consummation?

5. Why does the Roman Catholic Church insist that a marriage must take place in the presence of a priest and two witnesses to be valid? Does this make sense to you?

The Essence of Marriage:
The Continuing Search

In 1566, three years after the Council of Trent, Pope Pius V decreed the publication of the *Catechism of the Council of Trent for Priests.* It contained a section on the sacrament of matrimony, which advanced some notions of interest to us. First, marriage was defined as "the conjugal union of man and woman between legitimate persons, which is to last during life."[1] Secondly, it insisted that "marriage is not a simple donation, but a mutual contract."[2] Thirdly, it listed three goods associated with marriage, "offspring, faith and sacrament,"[3] and underscored the primacy of offspring over the others by insisting that "marriage, as a natural union, was instituted from the beginning for the propagation of the human race."[4] Over the next four hundred years, in their attempt to define what they called the *juridical essence* of marriage, canon lawyers of the Roman Church will ignore the first of these notions and concentrate exclusively on the other two. We shall reflect on how that happened and what it means.

The Code of Canon Law
and the Juridical Essence of Marriage

Gratian's *Decree* laid a foundation for the codification of the laws of the Catholic Church. That process took the next seven hundred years and reached its goal in the work of Cardinal Pietro Gasparri, the principal designer and editor of the *Code of Canon Law*, promulgated on Pentecost Sunday, 1917. Title VII of Book Three in that Code is entitled *De Matrimonio*, Concerning Marriage, and is largely inspired by Gasparri's most influential work, *Tractatus Canonicus de Matrimonio*, first published in 1892. Prominent in that work were three notions: first, marriage is a contract; secondly, the formal object of the contract is the permanent and exclusive mutual right of the spouses to each other's bodies for sexual intercourse; thirdly, the primacy of procreation over the other ends of marriage. These notions would control the Roman Catholic Church's approach to marriage questions until the Second Vatican Council.

Gasparri acknowledged that marriage was never called a contract either in Roman or in European law. But he insisted that it must be a contract since it is formed by two parties consenting to the same thing, thereby creating mutual obligations, just as a contract does. In an analysis of Gasparri's use of his sources for his judgment on the formal object of the contract, the mutual right of the spouses to each other's bodies, David Fellhauer shows that there is "no source which presents the juridical essence of marriage as the *jus in corpus* for procreation or which identifies the object of consent in similar terms."[5]

In a similar comprehensive analysis, Navarette demonstrates that "if we look at the documents of the Magisterium on marriage, or the documents of the Holy See in general, or the Corpus of Canon Law itself, which pertain somehow to this subject, we notice, not without surprise, that we find hardly anything about the ends of marriage precisely as goals until the formulation of Canon 1013,1 (in 1917)."[6] He points out further that in a preliminary formulation of Canon 1013 there was no indication of any hierarchy of ends. It read: "The end of marriage is not only the procreaton and nurture of children, but also mutual help and the remedy for concupiscence." Navarette concludes that the Code of Canon Law is the first document of the Roman Catholic Church to order hierarchically the ends of marriage and the first to use the terminology *primary end–secondary end.* It is not too difficult to see here an interpretative activity on the part of Gasparri nor, given his principal role in editing the first *Code of Canon Law*, is it surprising to see his interpretation showing up in the *Code.*

The opening canon on marriage firmly locates it as a contract. "Christ the Lord elevated the contract itself of marriage to the dignity of a sacrament" (Canon 1012,1). The same canon affirms also that in the case of the baptized, though the marriage contract and the marriage sacrament are distinguishable, they are not at all separable "Therefore, it is not possible that a valid marriage contract exist between baptized persons without being by that very fact a sacrament" (Canon 1012,2). This latter assertion was the end point of a long-running dispute between the Roman Church and emerging European states over who had authority in marriage. By asserting that contract and sacrament in the marriages of Christians are inseparable, the Church asserted its authority over not only sacraments but also the civil marriages of the baptized. By implication it was asserting also that any valid marriage contract between baptized persons is by that very fact also a sacrament. Not only does the *Code* establish the juridical essence of marriage as contract, but also it establishes the juridical essence of marrige as sacrament. I intend to challenge the reductionist simplicity of this in the next chapter.

There follows immediately the Gasparrian hierarchy of ends. "The primary end of marriage is the procreation and nurture of children; its secondary end is mutual help and the remedying of concupiscence" (Canon 1013,1). Implicit in this hierarchy of ends is also a subordination of ends; that is, since the ends are arranged as primary and secondary, in the case of any conflict between the ends the lesser or secondary value must always give way to the greater or primary. That subordinationism will control the discussion of all marriage questions in the years that followed the promulgation of the *Code.*

The long-established Roman opinion about what makes a marriage, an opinion we are already familiar with, is also enthroned in the *Code*. "Marriage is created by the consent of the parties legitimately expressed between persons capable of it by law" (Canon 1081,1). That "marital consent is an act of the will by which each party gives and accepts a perpetual and exclusive right over the body for acts which are of themselves suitable for the generation of children" (Canon 1081,2). So crucial is that consent and that formal object of consent that any absence of it whatever invalidates an attempted marriage. "In order that marital consent be possible, it is necessary that the contracting parties be, at least, not ignorant that marriage is a permanent society between a man and a woman for the procreation of children" (Canon 1082,1). "This ignorance is not presumed after puberty" (Canon 1082,2). So crucial is the right to the body of the other party that any effort to exclude it invalidates a marriage (Canon 1086,2).

A close reading of the 1917 *Code* yields a definition of the juridical essence of marriage not only as contract but also as sacrament (since, according to Canon 1012,2, they are inseparable in the marriages of baptized persons). This reductionist definition may be articulated this way. "Marriage the institution (marriage *in facto esse*) is a permanent society (Canon 1082), whose primary end is procreation and nurture (Canon 1013,1), a society that is in species a contract that is unitary and indissoluble by nature (Canon 1012 and Canon 1013,2), whose substance is the parties' exchanged right to their sexual acts (Canon 1081,2)."[7] That definition articulates the juridical essence of marriage which controlled the canonical arguments in Catholic courts up to the post-Vatican II era, but which has been displaced in our day in most courts throughout the Catholic world. I call it a reductionist definition, for while it carefully specifies what is included in the essence of marriage, it just as carefully specifies, at least implicitly, what is left out. It is precisely on this count that it was attacked and eventually replaced.

The Modern Development of the Juridical Essence

In December 1930, Pope Pius XI published his very important encyclical on Christian Marriage, *Casti Connubii*. In it, predictably, he insisted on everything we have seen in the juridical essence. But, quite unpredictably, he did more. He retrieved and gave a prime place to an ancient essence of marriage found as far back as the Letter to the Ephesians and as recently as the Catechism of the Council of Trent, the mutual love of husband and wife. If one considers only the canonical juridical definition, one could be forgiven for assuming that a man and woman who hate one another would with no difficulty be married, just as long as each gave to the other the right to his or her body. By emphasizing the essential place of mutual love in a marriage, Pius firmly rejected such nonsense and placed the Catholic view of marriage, however unwittingly, on a much more personal track.

This love, Pius teaches, does not consist

in pleasing words only, but in the deep attachment of the heart which is expressed in action, since love is proved by deeds. This outward expression of love in the home demands not only mutual help but must go further; must have as its primary purpose that man and wife help each other day by day in forming and perfecting themselves in the interior life, so that through their partnership in life they may advance ever more and more in virtue, and above all that they may grow in true love toward God and their neighbor, on which indeed "depends the whole law and the Prophets."

So important is this mutual interior formation of the spouses that "it can, in a very real sense, as the Roman catechism teaches, be said to be *the chief reason and purpose of matrimony*, if matrimony be looked at not in the restricted sense as instituted for the proper conception and education of the child, but more widely as the blending of life as a whole and the mutual interchange and sharing thereof."[8] In these wise words, Pius leads us to see that there is more to the essence of marriage than can be contained in the nice canonical categories of the reductionist juridical essence. This very same suggestion was about to be put forward by certain European thinkers.

The best known of those thinkers were two Germans, Dietrich von Hildebrand and Heribert Doms. In the opening paragraph of his work entitled *Marriage*, Von Hildebrand states clearly what he thinks the problem is:

Our epoch is characterized by a terrible anti-personalism, a progressive blindness toward the nature and dignity of the spiritual person. This anti-personalism expresses itself mainly in a radical collectivism and in the different kinds of materialism. Of these, biological materialism is perhaps the most dangerous, for it considers man as a more highly developed animal, his whole personality determined by mere physiological elements. Human life is considered exclusively from a biological point of view and biological principles are the measure by which all human activities are judged.[9]

Now the so-called juridical essence approach to marriage and sexual intercourse, with its insistence on rights over bodies and their biological actions, is wide open to the charge of biological materialism. So too is the centuries-old stoic-cum-Christian doctrine that argues from biological structure to "nature" and to "natural" ends. So too is Aquinas's position that the primary end of *human* marriage is rooted in man's *biological* nature. In contrast to these approaches, whatever one calls them, von Hildebrand introduced a radical innovation in thinking and talking about marriage. He considers it by itself, and not just as a means to attaining goods or ends outside itself. He claims Pius XI and his *Casti Connubii* in support of his central thesis that marriage exists so that the two spouses can build up conjugal community. Conjugal love, he says, is the ultimate end[10] and primary meaning of marriage.[11]

In marriage, the spouses enter into an interpersonal I-Thou relationship, in which they confront one another face to face and "give birth to a mysterious fusion of their souls."[12] This deeply personal fusion of their very beings, and not just the biological fusion of their bodies, is what the oft-quoted "one body" of Genesis intends. It is this interpersonal fusion that is the primary meaning of the spouses' sexual intercourse, and intercourse achieves its primary end when it leads to such fusion. "Every marriage in which conjugal love is thus realized bears spiritual fruit, becomes *fruitful*—even though there are no children."[13] The parentage of such thought in modern personalist philosophy is as clear as the parentage of the prior biological-natural thought in ancient Stoic philosophy. Even clearer, though, is the resonance of such a description of marriage and love-making with the lived experience of many married couples.

Doms brought to von Hildebrand's thought a more extended theory. He insisted, correctly I believe, that what is natural or unnatural for *human* animals is not to be decided on the basis of what is natural or unnatural for nonhuman animals. For humans are specifically spiritual animals, that is, animals vitalized by a spiritual soul. Sexual persons are not to be judged, as the Stoics and Aquinas judged them, against the backdrop of animal biology. For human sexuality is essentially the capacity and the desire to fuse, not only one's body, but especially one's whole personality with that of another person of differing sex. Sexuality drives a man to make a gift of himself (not merely of his body) to a woman (not just to her body) to form a community of persons and of lives which completes and fulfills each of them. In such a perspective, sexual intercourse is a powerful human and interpersonal activity in which a man gives himself to a woman and a woman gives herself to a man, and in which they mutually accept each other's gifts.

The primary end of intercourse in this perspective is precisely the mutual giving and accepting leading to conjugal union. This end is achieved, at least objectively, in every act of sexual intercourse, whereas other ends, such as the procreation of a child, are not always achieved. A child is without question the natural flowering of conjugal love, a gift of the spouses one to the other. But even in childless marriages, marriage and sexual intercourse achieve their end in the conjugal union of the spouses, their *two-in-oneness*, as Doms would have it. He prefers to lay to rest the terminology *primary end-secondary end*, because from one point of view one end might be primary and another secondary, while from another point of view the reverse might be the case. He summarizes his case in this statement. "The *immediate* purpose of marriage is the realization of its meaning, the conjugal two-in-oneness . . . This two-in-oneness of husband and wife is a living reality, and the immediate object of the marriage ceremony and their legal union. This vital two-in-oneness is to some extent a purpose in itself. It is for them a source of health and sanctity, and becomes for them the door to every natural and supernatural consummation. It tends also to the birth and education of new persons—their children. The child assists their own fulfillment, both as a two-in-oneness and as separate individuals. But society is more interested in the child than in the natural fulfillment of the parents, and it is this which gives the child primacy among the natural results of marriage."[14]

We shall see that Pope Paul VI agreed substantially with Doms, for in his influential encyclical, *Humanae Vitae*, he deals not with the *ends* of marriage but with its *meanings*. But that was much later. The Church's immediate reaction to these new ideas, as has so often been the case in its history, was to condemn them in blanket fashion, making no effort to sift the wheat from the chaff in Doms's position. The first condemnation came from the Holy Office in 1944. It answered in the negative this question, "Can one admit the opinion of some more recent authors, who either deny that the primary end of marriage is the generation and nurture of children, or teach that the secondary ends are not essentially subordinate to the primary end, but are equally primary and independent?"[15] Doms, of course, could claim that the Holy Office's condemnation did not refer to him since, as we have seen, he taught quite clearly that the terminology *primary end-secondary end* depends so much on perspective that one ought not even to use it. But, whether it missed his point or not, it condemned him and his efforts to advance the Church's teaching on marriage.

The Holy Office condemnation, while it removed Doms's work from the purview of Catholics, did not put an end to theological reflection on marriage in personalist themes. In 1951 Pope Pius XII felt obliged to intervene again. In an address to Italian Catholic Obstetricians, he drew attention to and condemned as false the personalist approach to marriage and its claims for the primacy of conjugal union over the procreation of children. While allowing that "if this relative evaluation were merely to accent the value of the persons of the spouses rather than that of the child, one could, strictly speaking, put the problem aside." But in this case that cannot be done, since there is in question "a serious inversion of values and ends imposed by the Creator himself." The truth is, he asserts, that

marriage, as a natural institution in virtue of the will of the Creator, does not have as a primary and intimate end the personal perfection of the spouses, but the procreation and nurture of new life. The other ends, in as much as they also are intended by nature, are not on the same level as the primary end, and still less are they superior to it, but they are essentially subordinate to it.[16]

The terms of the discussion could not be more precise. Are all other ends of marriage subordinate to procreation and nurture of new life (a hierarchy introduced to official church statements only by Gasparri), or are they at least of the same value as that end? It is a discussion that will continue up to, and beyond, the Second Vatican Council.

The Second Vatican Council and Marriage

"Before the Council, the Bishops had been sent a schema on 'Marriage, Family and Chastity.' Taken as a whole it was timeless and unproblematic. It was intended to perpetuate the negative and rigoristic casuistry of the standard textbooks. The events of the First Session of the Council made it perfectly clear that this schema could expect no better fate than the almost equally bad schema on the 'Sources of Revelation.' The Council was spared a discussion."[17] In these words, Bernhard Haring opens his commentary on Part 2, Chapter 1, of the *Pastoral Constitution on the Church in the Modern World.* We can assume with security that Haring is making his judgment on the badness of the Schema, not on the basis of some *a priori* personal preference, but on the *a posteriori* basis of its actual fate. Some background on that fate will serve to introduce a contemporary Roman Catholic approach to marriage.

Following the announcement of the calling of an Ecumenical Council, a Central Preparatory Commission was established to receive, edit, and distribute documents to be discussed in the plenary sessions of the Council. Early in 1962 that Central Commission received from a Theological Commission chaired by Cardinal Ottaviani, then Prefect of the Holy Office, a schema entitled *De Castitate, Virginitate, Matrimonio, Familia.* It discussed the schema in May 1962, and overwhelmingly rejected it. A sampling from the schema will illustrate two things. First, it will demonstrate the "negative and rigorous casuistry" which characterized the document. Secondly, it will allow us to demarcate what was rejected, both in the Preparatory Commission and again in the Council, as a contemporary Roman Catholic approach to marriage.

Along with the schema, Cardinal Ottaviani had sent the Central Commission a note of explanation. "Before all else the Theological Commission has set out the objective order, that is, that which God himself willed in instituting marriage, and Christ the Lord willed in raising it to the dignity of sacrament. Only in this way can the modern errors that have spread everywhere be vanquished."[18] Among those errors are "those theories which subvert the right order of values and make the primary end of marriage inferior to the biological and personal values of the spouses, and proclaim that conjugal love itself is in the objective order the primary end."[19] The schema offers the hierarchy of ends traditional since Gasparri. "The one and only primary end is the procreation and nurture of children. . . . The other objective ends of marriage, rooted in the character itself of marriage but still secondary—such as the spouses' mutual help and the remedying of concupiscence—constitute genuine, even if subordinate, rights in marriage when they are rightly intended."[20] The debate, both the preliminary one in the Central Commission and the decisive one in the Council itself, centered around the hierarchy of ends, and specifically around the relative values of conjugal love and the procreation of children. I do not intend here to detail the history of that debate but, for the requirements of this book, only its outcome as it is revealed to us in the finished Part 2, Chapter 1, of the *Pastoral Constitution on the Church in the Modern World.*[21]

Marriage is described in that Constitution as a "community of love" (n.47), an "intimate partnership of conjugal life and love" (n.48). The Council's position could not be clearer. In the face of strident demands to downplay the conjugal love of the spouses, it declared that love to be of the very essence of marriage. The intimate partnership of life and love is rooted in a "conjugal covenant of irrevocable personal consent" (n.48). Again, when faced with demands to retain the juridical and Gasparrian word *contract* as a precise way to speak of marriage, the Council demurred, and chose instead the more biblical word *covenant.* This choice firmly locates marriage as a *personal,* rather than an exclusively *legal,* reality and brings it into line with the covenant relationship between Christ and his Church. The interpersonal character of the marrriage covenant is further underscored by the choice, again in the face of a chorus of demands to the contrary, of a way to characterize the formal object of the covenanting. The Council declares that the spouses "mutually gift and accept one another" (n.48), rejecting the reductionist notion that they gift merely the right to one another's bodies. This mutual gifting and accepting creates an institution which is not merely a temporary one, until love ends, for instance, but a permanent one, one which "no longer depends on human actions alone" (n.48).

The Council emphasizes that both the institution of marriage and the marital love of the spouses "are ordained for the procreation and education of children, and find in them their ultimate crown" (n.48). But, again despite insistent voices to the contrary, it refused to employ the primary end-secondary end terminology when it spoke of the ends of marriage. Indeed the Preparatory Commission was careful to state explicitly that the text just quoted "does not suggest this (that is, a hierarchy of ends) in any way."[22] The Council states that "marriage and conjugal love are by their nature ordained to the generation and education of children," but again insists that this "does not make the other purposes of marriage of less account" (n.50), and that marriage "is not instituted solely for procreation" (n.50). The intense debate that took place both in the Central Commission and in the sessions of the Council itself makes it impossible to claim that the refusal to speak of a hierarchy of ends in marriage was the result of any oversight or lapse of memory. There can be no doubt that it was the result of a quite deliberate and documentable choice. Conjugal love is an end of marriage; the procreation of children is an end of marriage; in the 1960s, the Roman Catholic Church meeting in Council refused to rank these two ends.

The most recent formal statement of the Church on marriage is in its revised *Code of Canon Law* which came into force on the first day of Advent, 1983. That *Code*, which selectively embodies only some of the recent developments in the doctrine of Christian marriage, nevertheless makes significant changes to the *Code* which came into force in 1917, all of them in line with the doctrine initiated by Vatican II. The first canon on marriage sets the tone which will continue through the entire Title. "The marriage covenant, by which a man and a woman establish between themselves a partnership of their whole life, and which of its very nature is ordered to the well-being of the spouses and to the procreation and upbringing of children, has, between the baptized, been raised by Christ the Lord to the dignity of a sacrament" (Canon 1055,1).

Gone is the word *contract*, introduced by Gasparri, replaced, as in the Council, by the biblical word *covenant*. A contract deals with things; a covenant deals with persons. A contract deals with legal things, like a man's right over a woman's body and vice versa, and so that too is gone. Marriage is still "brought into being by the lawfully manifested consent of persons who are legally capable" (Canon 1057,1), but that consent "is an act of the will by which a man and a woman by irrevocable covenant mutually give and accept *one another* for the purpose of establishing a marriage" (Canon 1057,2). Gone too is the hierarchy of ends, again as in the Council, and as in Paul VI's *Humanae Vitae*, which appeared just two and a half years after the council adjourned. Of its very nature, marriage "is ordered to the well-being of the spouses and to the procreation and upbringing of children," with no evaluation as to which of these is primary or secondary. The Catholic Church has changed its law to be in line with its theology of marriage. It has moved beyond the narrow juridical essence to include in the essence of marriage realities which the juridical essence excluded. Chief among these realities is the conjugal love and community of wife and husband.

On October 30, 1970, the Roman Rota, the Supreme Marriage Tribunal of the Roman Catholic Church, delivered a decision in a marriage case which illustrates this momentous shift in perspective. It ruled that "where conjugal love is lacking, either the consent is not free, or it is not internal, or it excludes or limits the object which must be integral to have a valid marriage." It concluded that "lack of conjugal love is the same as lack of consent. Conjugal love has juridical force here, because the defendant despised the total communion of life which primarily and of itself constitutes the object of the marriage contract."[23] Lack of conjugal love, according to this Rotal decision, is the same as lack of consent. If a marriage cannot be a valid marriage without free consent, neither can it be a valid marriage without conjugal love. Once upon a time, in his magisterial *Church Dogmatics*, Karl Barth complained that the traditional Christian doctrine of marriage, both Catholic and Protestant, dealt with marriage in juridical rather than in theological categories, and despised love between the spouses.[24] In our time, the Roman Catholic Church, at least, has corrected that grave imbalance. Armed with that information, we can now proceed to what this book is about—namely systematic reflection on a contemporary Catholic theology of Christian marriage.

Summary

This chapter has been about one thing: the essence of Christian marriage as it has been conceived in the Roman Catholic Church since the Council of Trent. It has sought to document the shift that has taken place in the understanding of that essence, a shift that is from an exclusively biological, called natural, base to a personal one. That shift is evidenced in three related instances. First, the treatment of marriage is no longer in the Gasparri-introduced category of *contract* which deals with things, but in the biblically-rooted category of *covenant* which deals with persons. Secondly, the object of consent in a marriage is viewed no longer in the Gasparri-inspired terms of mutual biological rights over bodies, but in terms of the mutual personal gifts of the spouses to one another to form a community of love. Thirdly, this mutual love of the spouses is no longer subordinated to the procreation of children, but is stated to be a good of marriage, at least, equal to the good of procreation. We recall that, if Navarette is right, the terminology *primary end-secondary end* was introduced into an official document of the Roman Catholic Church only in the *Code of Canon Law* in 1917 and can hardly be said, therefore, to be traditional.

Questions for Reflection and Discussion

1. Do you look upon marriage as a contract or a covenant? What pros and cons do you see in both approaches?

2. Did you know that the *Code of Canon Law* described the object of the marriage contract as the spouses' mutual rights over the other's body? Does that seem to you an adequate way to describe marriage as you understand it?

3. That emphasis on mutual rights over bodies has been replaced in the new *Code* by an emphasis on the mutual gifting of persons. Do you believe that this movement from biological to personal emphasis diminishes or enhances your view of Christian marriage? Explain.

4. If theological theory undergoes a shift from describing the ends of marriage, procreation and the mutual help of the spouses, as primary and secondary to describing them as equal, what is the result? In your married life, where would such a shift have any practical effect?

5. In your opinion, is it for the good of marriage that the Roman Rota, the supreme court of the Roman Catholic Church, is now treating the presence of love in marriage with the same seriousness as it treats the presence of free consent? Where, do you think, will such an emphasis have the most effect?

Theology of Marriage:
A Contemporary Catholic View

I begin this elaboration of a contemporary Catholic theology of marriage by reflecting on two ecclesiastical decisions which shaped that theology. The first is the settlement of the dispute about whether marriage is constituted by consent or by subsequent sexual intercourse. That settlement, we recall, was in favor of consent. The second is Trent's decision in *Tametsi* to require for valid consent that it be made in the presence of a priest and two witnesses. These two decisions delivered marriage into the domain of those expert in the giving and the receiving of consent, lawyers. Their legitimate professional concerns for legality and validity dominated discussion about marriage in the doctrinal and moral textbooks from the Council of Trent until the

Second Vatican Council. They also dominated lectures, sermons, and ecclesiastical pronouncements about marriage. However necessary such moral-canonical niceties might have been, and I believe them to have been necessary as long as the essence of marriage was conceived in juridical terms, they still left couples bemused and asking what any of them had to do with their experience of love and marriage.

The *Code of Canon Law* is the source of more confusion. The 1917 version states: 1) "the consent of the parties, legitimately manifested before persons capable of receiving it, makes marriage"; and 2) "Christ the Lord raised the marriage contract between baptized persons to the dignity of sacrament. Therefore, there cannot be a valid marriage contract between baptized persons without it being, by that very fact, a sacrament" (Canons 1081,1 and 1012, 1 and 2). These statements, repeated in the revised version of 1983 (cf. Can. 1055 and 1057), give rise to several problems, which in turn yield insight into other problems which face Christian marriage.

Some Problems

One problem is that to insist exclusively that legitimately manifested consent makes marriage, however true that may be as a legal statement about marriage *in fieri*, as the classical language would say, is to run the risk of ignoring the importance of marriage *in facto esse*. It is the latter that most married, and even the most naive of about-to-be-married, couples experience as their marriage, as distinct from their wedding. It is the latter also, I would dare to say especially, that is the sacrament of marriage. That means that it is a married life, much more than a marriage ceremony, that is both the prophetic symbol which proclaims and makes real and celebrates in representation the community between Christ and his Church and the life situation in which married men and women encounter Christ and God and grace. There is an old aphorism in marriage counseling which gets closer to the heart of both secular and sacramental marriage than does the *Code*. When are two people married? Thirty years later! It is a true, if cute, answer to the question, which would wither in an atmosphere of legal scrutiny. For the moment I am content to say that, in the warm glow of human scrutiny, it comes closer to what couples experience in their marriage, that becoming married, becoming two in one body, becoming sacramental symbol of the great covenant is a much more continuous activity than simply giving consent in two little words, "I do."

A second problem, perhaps even a series of problems, with the Church's exclusively legalistic approach to marriage and sacrament arises in an ambiguity created by apparently conflicting claims. On the one hand, there is the *Code's* claim that legitimate consent makes marriage and, in the case of the baptized, makes sacrament. This claim would seem to lead to the twofold conclusion that consent, however manifested, makes valid marriage and, in the case of the baptized, that such valid marriages are sacraments. The first part of the conclusion leads to conflict with the claim of the Church that marriage is indissoluble. If consent makes valid marriage and if a valid marriage is indissoluble, how can the Church dissolve the valid marriages of non-baptized persons so that they, now baptized, may enter into a sacramental marriage? The second part of the conclusion either is called into question by, or calls into question, the theory and practice deriving from *Tametsi*, which decrees that for baptized persons any consent to marry not given before a priest and two witnesses does not lead to a valid marriage and, therefore, not to a valid sacrament. The Tridentine decree introduces an element, quite extrinsic to the contract, and requires it for the validity of both legal contract and the religious sacrament—a situation which appears to conflict with the *Code's* simple claim that legitimately manifested consent makes marriage.

One might argue, of course, that as social institution the Church is quite free and within its rights to establish whatever form of signifying consent it chooses. I do not doubt or challenge that right. I wish only to point out that it fails to come to grips with the fact that a practice introduced historically to root out clandestine marriages and to protect the sacrament of marriage now impinges on the human right to marry and to manifest consent in some form other than the Tridentine.

There remains one final and major problem with the *Code's* view of marriage and sacrament. To stress exclusively the identity between the contract of marriage and the sacrament of marriage runs the risk of ignoring what is specific to *Christian* marriage. Every marriage in the Western world is constituted by consent. When all that is required for Christian marriage is that Christians give the same consent given in all marriages, even if in a different form, it is not too difficult for couples to get the impression that Christian marriage is just like any other marriage, except that it is between Christians. It is easy for them, and for the pastors who minister to them, to focus so exclusively on the giving of consent that they forget about the married life that both follows from that consent and is its ongoing concretization.

It might be this impression that Christian marriage is no different from any other marriage that is the cause of the present situation in which so many Christian marriages are, in fact, quite indistinguishable from other marriages. It might be this very same impression and this very same situation in which so-called Christian marriages are indistinguishable from other marriages that are the reasons why so many young Christians, insisting truly that they love one another, and not quite so truly that all you need is love, find the religious ritualizing of their already-given mutual consent so trivial and, in the end, irrelevant. To declare, indiscriminately, that they are lacking in faith seems to me to be too sweeping a statement to be true. I believe that the problem derives not so much from any lack of faith on their part as from the view of marriage that is offered to them in the legal definitions of the *Code*, a view that does not allow them to suspect that their personal faith has anything to do with it. But, of course, as a long tradition of the Church teaches, personal faith has everything to do with Christian sacrament. It has everything to do, therefore, with *Christian* marriage.

Faith and Sacrament

One cannot but be impressed, on reading the New Testament, with its emphasis on faith as a means of salvation. Jesus complained insistently of the absence of faith. Paul defended vehemently the necessity of personal faith against the legalism of the Judaizers. Juan Alfaro explains what that faith meant and means. It "includes knowledge of a saving event, confidence in the word of God, man's humble submission and personal self-surrender to God, fellowship in life with Christ, and a desire for perfect union with him beyond the grave. Faith is man's comprehensive 'Yes' to God's revealing himself as man's savior in Christ."[1]

The primacy of this faith in the process of salvation was acknowledged and affirmed as a Catholic tradition by the Council of

Trent. "We may be said to be justified through faith, in the sense that 'faith is the beginning of man's salvation,' the foundation and source of all justification, 'without which it is impossible to please God' (Hebrews 11:6) and to be counted as his sons."[2] The same idea was reiterated in the important chapter on justification, where it was stated that the instrumental cause of a sinner's justification is "the sacrament of baptism which is the 'sacrament of faith,' without which no man has ever been justified."[3] The Latin text leaves no room for doubt that the phrase "without which no man has ever been justified" refers to faith. *Without which* renders the Latin *sine qua*, which as it stands can refer only to the feminine word *faith*. If it referred to the masculine word *baptism* or to the neuter word *sacrament*, it would have to be *sine quo*.[4] There is no possible doubt that the Fathers at Trent wanted fervently to affirm the primacy of faith in the question of justification.

The Council of Trent taught also that sacraments confer the grace they signify on the person who presents no obstacle.[5] It opted for this minimalistic formulation to cover in one rule the cases of both children and adults, and it applies positively only to the case of children. In the prior Council of Florence, the Roman tradition had already carefully specified that for an adult placing no obstacle meant having a positive, personal intent. The sacraments, it taught, give grace only to those who receive them worthily.[6] This doctrine demands an active, positive disposition of self-surrendering faith on the part of the one participating in a sacramental action. Such a doctrine makes a sacrament a true *sign of faith*, that is, a sign not only of the faith of the Church which seeks to proclaim and make real and celebrate in prophetic symbol and sacrament the presence of God and his Christ, but also of the believer who concelebrates that presence with the Church.

Vatican Council II underscores that position as the truly Catholic position. It teaches that sacraments "not only presuppose faith" but "also nourish, strengthen and express it," which "is why they are called 'sacraments of faith.'"[7] The Catholic position is, and always has been, clear: fruitful sacramental activity presupposes faith. A believer comes to sacramental action in and with faith, and with that faith transforms ordinary, simple human actions and words into prophetic symbols and sacraments. As Aquinas would say: the saving action of God and Christ "achieves its effect in those to whom

it is applied through faith and love and the sacraments of faith."[8]
Personal faith, a believer's comprehensive 'Yes' to God, what the
Medievals called *opus operantis*, is as essential to any fruitful sacrament as the most carefully crafted *opus operatum* or sacramental
action.

There is a serious doctrinal flaw, therefore, in both the 1917
Code and the 1983 revision. To claim that consent makes marriage is
true as a legal and canonical statement; there is no marriage, neither
secular nor sacramental, without it. To claim that secular marriage
created by mutual consent is transformed into prophetic symbol and
sacrament is true as a statement of the faith of the Church. But to
claim that secular marriage is transformed to be prophetic symbol
and sacrament by each and every baptized Christian requires a major
distinction: by those who share the faith of the Church, yes; by those
who do not share the faith of the Church, no. No one is graced and
justified without faith, not even in sacraments, not even in the sacrament of Christian marriage. A long-standing principle of Roman
Catholic sacramental theology has been that sacraments are essentially "sacraments of faith," requiring for their fruitfulness a minimal
contribution of active faith on the part of the person receiving them.
What I have just argued is merely the specification of this general
sacramental principle to marriage: in marriage only Christian faith
makes the difference between universal human reality and *Christian*
sacrament.

Secular Marriage—Christian Sacrament

The Fathers of Vatican II, as we have seen already, never used the legal
word *contract* of marriage, but preferred the much more biblical and
personal word *covenant*. Marriage, they taught, "is rooted in the
conjugal covenant of irrevocable personal consent."[9] That notion of
marriage as a covenant transformed the ecclesiastical approach to
marriage and passed into the law of the Church in the 1983 Code of
Canon Law. There, where the 1917 Code had spoken of "the marriage
contract," Canon 1055,1, speaks of "the marriage covenant." Canon
1057,2 explains that "matrimonial consent is an act of the will by which
a man and a woman by an irrevocable covenant mutually give and
accept one another for the purpose of establishing a marriage." Some

brief reflection on the distinction between contract and covenant will show the way in which the Catholic theology of marriage has changed in our day.

I have already hinted at the direction of the change by describing covenant as a more "biblical and personal" word. Paul Palmer has sought to clarify the meaning of covenant more explicitly by contrasting it with contract. He deserves to be cited in full.

Contracts deal with things, covenants with people. Contracts engage the services of people; covenants engage persons. Contracts are made for a stipulated period of time; covenants are forever. Contracts can be broken, with material loss to the contracting parties; covenants cannot be broken, but if violated, they result in personal loss and broken hearts. Contracts are secular affairs and belong to the market place; covenants are sacral affairs and belong to the hearth, the temple or the church. Contracts are best understood by lawyers, civil and ecclesiastical; covenants are appreciated better by poets and theologians. Contracts are witnessed by people with the state as guarantor; covenants are witnessed by God with God as guarantor. Contracts can be made by children who know the value of a penny; covenants can be made only by adults who are mentally, emotionally, and spiritually mature.[10]

I believe that all these distinctions are supremely true. I believe also that they will help us see that the heart of marriage lies not in its being a contract, but in its being an interpersonal covenant and community of love which is permanent and exclusive. They will help us further to distinguish clearly between *Christian* marriage and all other marriages.

Vatican II again gives us the lead, in terms that Augustine, Gregory and Aquinas could never have written. It declares that marriage, a "community of love," an "intimate partnership of married life and love," a "mutual gift of two persons," is "a reflection of the loving covenant uniting Christ with the church," and "a participation in that covenant."[11] There is, first, the steadfastly loving covenant of the Old Law, uniting Yahweh and his people; there is, secondly, the steadfastly loving covenant of the New Law, uniting Christ and his Church; there is, thirdly, the steadfastly loving covenant of Christian marriage, uniting a man and a woman, which reflects, participates in, and extends the other two.

In every symbol there are two levels of meaning, a literal, foundational one, and a symbolic one built on this foundation. On the foundational level, for instance, water bespeaks life and death, which makes it wonderfully apt to express such meanings as it does in baptism. Christian marriage has the same two levels of meaning. There is the foundational loving community of this man and this woman. Built on this foundation, there is the symbolic representation and reflection of the loving community of Christ and his Church. In *Christian* marriage there is proclaimed, made real, and celebrated, not only the mutual love of the spouses, but also the love of Christ for his Church.

In Christian marriage, in fact, the symbolic meaning takes precedence, in the sense that the love of Christ is the model for the mutual love of husband and wife. Besides, as a Christian husband and a Christian wife love one another in marriage, they are not just this husband and this wife loving one another. They are also the Church in microcosm, "the domestic church" Vatican II calls them,[12] believing in and loving its Lord. This is what it means to say that Christian marriage participates in the covenant uniting Christ and his Church. This is what it means to say that Christian marriage is graced, that is God and Christ are present in it, providing the models of steadfast love on which it is based, strengthening it and making the spouses holy by their presence. But the covenant of marriage is graced under the very same condition as the covenants it reflects. "If you will obey my voice and keep my covenant, you shall be my own possession among all peoples" (Exodus 19:4) expresses the condition of grace under the Old Covenant. "Love the Lord your God with all your heart, and with all your soul, and with all your mind. . . . Love your neighbor as yourself" (Matthew 22:37–40) expresses the condition of grace under the New Covenant. "Love your neighbor as yourself" is equally the condition of grace in the covenant of Christian marriage. So necessary is this love between the spouses that the Roman Rota is now willing to declare null and void a marriage in which it was lacking from the beginning.

The key that opens the door to such covenant meanings is not just the mutual consent of the spouses to marry, but rather their Christian faith which impels them to consent to represent Church, Christ, and God. Consent may make a marriage a secular institution, but it is faith that makes it also Christian sacrament. Such an approach to secular marriage as also religious covenant and sacrament has serious implications for ecclesiastical courts. For centuries such courts have been delivering judgments on the validity or nonvalidity of marriages and, as we shall see in the next chapter, today they are delivering judgments of nonvalidity in ever-growing numbers. None of those judgments is based on a defective faith, however, but on a defective consent or defective covenant love. Could that be changed? Could a secular social institution, constituted by mutual consent, and Christian sacrament, constituted by mutual consent and Christian faith, be not only distinguishable but also separable, so that a couple, even a baptized couple, could have one without the other? That question, predictably, provokes a wide range of answers from lawyers and theologians. I do not intend to survey those answers here.[13] I intend only to consider two problems intimately related to the question and to one another. There is, first, the problem involved in claiming that every marriage between baptized persons is a sacrament. There is, secondly, the problem of claiming that every marriage between baptized persons not celebrated in the form decreed by *Tametsi* is not a sacrament, not even a valid marriage, and therefore concubinage or living in sin. Both problems are so intimately related that any statement about the one will be *eo ipso* a statement about the other.

A possible counterclaim must be disposed of at the outset. The Council of Trent states emphatically: "If anyone says that *marriage* is not one of the seven sacraments . . . Let him be anathema."[14] The 1917 *Code* states equally emphatically: "Christ the Lord raised the *marriage contract between baptized persons* to the dignity of sacrament. Therefore, there cannot be a valid *marriage contract between baptized persons* without it being, by that very fact, a sacrament" (Canon 1012,2). The 1983 *Code* makes the same statement (Canon 1055,2). Notice the quite different language of the doctrinal and the canonical statements, the former asserting that *marriage* is a sacrament, the latter that the *marriage contract between baptized persons* is a sacrament. The two are vastly different claims.

In a careful analysis of the notions of contract and sacrament at the Council of Trent, Father A. Duval points out that it was not by some oversight that Trent said simply *marriage* and not something like *marriage between baptized persons*, but by quite deliberate choice. It wished to leave open a debate that the theology of the time could not resolve. "Canon 1 of the Council wishes to affirm the existence in the New Law of *a* sacrament of marriage—but not that marriage in the New Law is always a sacrament."[15] Far from declaring, even implicitly, the inseparability of contract and sacrament, the

Council chose quite deliberately to leave the question open. And the expansion in the *Code*, from *marriage* to *marriage contract between baptized persons*, may not be considered an explanation, and still less an authentic interpretation, of Trent's words.

The debate over the inseparability of contract and sacrament in marriage continued after Trent. In the nineteenth century it took a quite political twist. An attempt was made to distinguish between the marriage contract and the sacrament of marriage in order to give jurisdiction over the former to civil authority and jurisdiction over the latter to the Church. Both Pius IX and Leo XIII issued careful statements against such an approach. In 1852 Pius proclaimed that "there can be no marriage between *the faithful* without it being at the same time a sacrament."[16] In his encyclical letter of 1880, *Arcanum Divinae Sapientiae*, Leo taught that "in *Christian* marriage contract cannot be dissociated from sacrament."[17] Notice the much more precise language of these pontiffs as contrasted to that of the *Code*: marriage between the faithful, Christian marriage, rather than the very general marriage contract between baptized persons. Again, the *Code* cannot be advanced as an authentic explanation of what the popes intended in their official teaching.

The *Code*'s more general formulation was introduced by our old friend, Gasparri.[18] But neither his nor its general formulation binds the Council of Trent, nor the pontiffs who seemed to wish to be as careful as Trent, to an interpretation which was explicitly avoided. Since there has been no solemn Church teaching on the question since Trent, the Council's position remains still the official, dogmatic position of the Roman Church. There is *a* sacrament of marriage in the New Law, but not every marriage in the New Law is necessarily a sacrament. It is easier, of course, for the law to presume that every such marriage is a sacrament, but legal presumption does not constitute a sacrament. Only the real presence of the personal requisites does that. With the Catholic tradition I hold that only that church-offered sacrament approached in personal faith is personally-accepted sacrament and that, therefore, only that marriage approached in Christian faith is Christian sacramental marriage. That marriage, on the other hand, in which there is mutual consent but no transforming faith, even if it be between those who have been baptized, is valid marriage and not just concubinage, but is not valid sacrament.

Another possible counterargument is also based on a presumption. The *Code*'s identification of contract and sacrament in a marriage between baptized persons derives from a traditional Catholic understanding that baptism gives persons the gift of faith and makes them believers. That understanding is a little ambiguous, for the word *faith* in the tradition is ambiguous. It may refer either to what is known as the virtue of faith, the power or the know-how to make an act of faith, or to the actual act of faith itself. The virtue or know-how is a necessary prerequisite for the positing of the act, but the act does not follow necessarily and ineluctably from the know-how. I may have the know-how to drive an automobile, but that in itself is no guarantee that I will ever drive one. The Catholic tradition holds that it is the virtue of faith that is gifted in baptism.[19] Before that virtue may be imputed to anyone it must be activated freely, consciously, and deliberately into an actual act of faith. It is that personal act of faith that transforms both the human being into a Christian believer and human marriage into Christian, sacramental marriage. Sadly, our times have brought to the forefront of Christian consciousness a new phenomenon of countless numbers all over the world who have received the virtue of faith in baptism, but who have never made a personal act of faith in the God made known in Jesus. They comprise an anomalous brand of baptized persons, those who though baptized remain all their lives nonbelievers. These *baptized nonbelievers*[20] ought not be be equated with Catholic faithful in Catholic law.

Baptism does not give faith nor make believers in any but a very passive sense, namely, it gives the know-how to faith and to being a believer. The *Code*'s sweeping assumption that the Church is dealing with Christian believers from the moment of baptism, and that therefore every valid marriage between baptized persons is by that very fact a sacrament, is a rather simplistic, theologically naive assumption, and one that is manifestly false in countless cases in our day. It is difficult, no doubt, to assess the faith or nonfaith of any baptized person. It is my contention that the Christian sacramentality of marriages coincides with the range of faith and runs from sacramentality to non-sacramentality. The shades between the extremes may be difficult to assess, but no legal presumption will ever supply the lack of theological faith and consequent lack of theological sacramentality. Those who marry without Christian faith, be they ever so baptized, whether they marry with or without the prescribed canonical form, marry indeed validly and do not live in concubinage, but they do not marry sacramentally.[21]

Marriage is a gift of the Creator-God, who created man and woman differently so that they could love one another, join in a community of love called marriage, and become one whole person. I believe the time has come for Catholic theology to assert, in keeping with its own ancient tradition, the inalienable validity of every human marriage constituted by proper consent, including the validity of the marriages of the baptized outside the Tridentine form. It is in keeping with its own ancient tradition because it was the practice of the Catholic Church up to the Council of Trent and continues to be its practice today in situations where a priest may not easily be present.[22] The politico-historical struggle of the Church in eighteenth- and nineteenth-century Europe to assert its rights, against the rights of emerging civil authorities, over the marriages of Christians has been sufficiently won for it to start again taking seriously its own sacred tradition.

For many centuries the Catholic Church taught what it continues to teach today: consent makes marriage. The introduction of the present canonical form by *Tametsi* was aimed at eliminating the social and religious problems created by the plague of clandestine marriages. It is not inconceivable that similar problems could arise in our times. Indeed, people living together without being legally married, and the "palimony" problems created by the break-up of such unions, may be sign enough that they have arisen already. But they could be obviated by any publicly witnessed ritual; an ecclesiastically-witnessed ritual is not at all indispensable for a valid human marriage. The Church, then, could get on with its business of witnessing Christian sacrament. This would seem to have been the thinking of the Catholic bishops in France, introduced in the preface, who instructed their priests to urge baptized nonbelievers to marry in a civil ceremony and to seek a Church ceremony only if they were interested in the Christian sacrament of marriage.[23]

Explicitly acknowledging what I have argued about the relation of Christian sacrament to Christian faith, and recognizing that the marriages of nonbelievers are *ipso facto* non-sacramental, the French bishops asserted that such nonbelievers do not need the blessing of the Church to make valid human marriage. This would seem also to be the intent of the decree of Pope Paul VI, establishing that "when Eastern or Latin Catholics enter into marriage with Eastern non-Catholics, in such marriages the canonical form of celebration obliges only for legality; for validity the presence of a sacred minister is enough."[24] It is to be hoped fervently that this decision will be extended to allow new canonical rites of marriage, particularly for peoples in the third world in keeping with their own authentic marriage customs. That would be a remarkable sign that the Catholic Church is becoming a truly world Church, as distinct from an exclusively European one.

Such decisions would seem to be well in line with the twenty-year-old proclamation by Vatican II on the independence of earthly affairs. "Created things and societies themselves enjoy their own laws and values which must be gradually deciphered, put to use, and regulated by men."[25] Human marriage is one of those created realities that enjoys its own meanings and values apart from the Church. To acknowledge that simple fact would free marriage to be a truly human reality which, in its very created humanness, can become the basis for the sacrament of covenent marriage. It would be in line also with the Church's announced willingness "to renounce the exercise of legitimately acquired rights if it becomes clear that their use raises doubts about the sincerity of her witness or that new conditions of life demand some other arrangement."[26] It is, of course, my argument, and apparently also that of some bishops in France, that in the case of marriages, even of the baptized, new conditions have certainly arisen that demand another arrangement. The arrangement I have suggested is one which would be well in line also with the magnificent words of the Catholic Church on religious freedom. "It is one of the major tenets of Catholic doctrine that man's response to God *in faith* must be free. Therefore, no one is to be forced to embrace the Christian faith against his will. . . . in matters religious *every* manner of coercion on the part of men should be excluded."[27] It is hard to see how a Church that proclaims and believes in such an exalted vision could continue to deprive the baptized, believers and nonbelivers alike, of a right to secular marriage, a human reality for which they were created by God.

Christian Marriage as Sacrament

Every Catholic over thirty, and maybe even a few under thirty, knows the Tridentine definition of sacrament. "A sacrament is an outward sign of inward grace instituted by Christ." I would like to offer to all of them another definition. A sacrament is a prophetic symbol with which the Church, the Body of Christ, proclaims and makes real and celebrates for believers that presence and action of God which is called grace. If Christian marriage is a sacrament, and as a Catholic theologian I accept it as a given that it is, then it is such a prophetic symbol. In this section, therefore, only one question is at issue: what specific presence and action of God, what grace, is proclaimed and made real and celebrated by Christian believers in a Christian marriage? A complete answer to this question requires that we constantly keep in mind two quite distinct prophetic actions in Christian marriage. There is, first, the action ritualized in the wedding ceremony, the action of mutual consent "by which a man and a woman by an irrevocable covenant mutually give and accept one another for the purpose of establishing a marriage" (CIC,1983,1057,2). There is, secondly, and perhaps more crucially, the action of living that conjugal covenant in an "intimate partnership of married life and love." In ordinary language, both these actions are called *marriage*. In theological language, both deserve to be called *sacrament*. It is the meaning of this latter statement that I intend to elucidate here.

The *Code*'s statement is now well known to us. "The marriage covenant . . . has, between the baptized, been raised by Christ the Lord to the dignity of a sacrament"(CIC,1983, Canon 1055,1). From our biblical analysis in the opening chapter, particularly from our treatment of the Old Testament prophet, Hosea, and of the New Testament writer of the Letter to the Ephesians, we know of the prophetic symbol. It is an ordinary human action, like Jeremiah's dashing a pot to the ground (19:1-13) or Ezekiel's scattering his shorn hair to the winds (5:1-6), which proclaims and makes real and celebrates a deeper, more sacred reality. To say that the marriage covenant between a man and a woman is a sacrament is to say that it is such a prophetic symbol. It is to say that the marriage between this Christian man and this Christian woman is a two-tiered reality. The first, human tier proclaims and makes real and celebrates the intimate community between this man and this woman. The second, religious tier proclaims and celebrates, in both the Jewish and the Christian traditions, the steadfast covenant and loving community between Yahweh and his holy people, Israel, and between Christ and his holy people, the Church.

A couple entering into a secular marriage say to one another: "I love you and give myself [*myself*, not just *my body*, as the *Code* infamously said] to you." A Christian couple entering into the covenant of Christian marriage are saying that, but they are also saying much more: "I love you as myself, as God loves his people and as Christ loves his church." From the first, this marriage is more than just the union of this man and this woman. It is a religious covenant; from the first, God and his Christ are present as parties involved in it, modeling it, gracing it, and guaranteeing it. This presence of grace in its most ancient and solemn Christian sense, as the presence of the gracious God, is not extrinsic to the covenant. It is something essential to it, something without which it would not be *Christian* at all. Christian marriage does proclaim the love of this man and this woman; it also proclaims and makes real and celebrates their love for their God and their Christ. It is a sacrament, a sign, and a cause of inward grace.

The mutual love of husband and wife in a Christian marriage is not just any love, but love that is modeled on and reflects and is sustained by the love of God. It is *hesed*, steadfast love. Such a love is not difficult to promise; it is difficult to deliver over the long haul. When two believers have promised such love in a marriage ceremony, they have nothing left but to live it in married life. Both the ceremony and the life are marriage, and as Christian marriage manifest the covenant love of this couple and the covenant love of Christ for his Church. It is an exalted claim to make for Christian marriage, but it is the claim the Church makes when it declares that Christian marriage is a sacrament, and it is the claim that two Christians make when they claim they are entering into a specifically *Christian* marriage. For most of us married couples, Christian and non-Christian alike, it is a claim that is extraordinarily difficult to live by, because it is extraordinarily difficult for two ever to become one blood person.

In the human animal I distinguish three levels of being and action, which I shall designate as the physical, the psychological, and the spiritual. The physical is the level of biology and physiology; it is the level that humans share with others in the genus *animal*. The psychological is the level of sense and imagination and memory and understanding and reason and judgment and emotion; it is the level that is specific to the *human* animal. The spiritual is the level of all that transcends the physical and the psychological, all that transcends the animal and the merely human, all that reaches within to the depths and without to the beyond of the human; it is the level which only the *religious* animal, in the broadest meaning of religious, attains.[28] To become one biblical body, one whole person, a man and a woman must become one on all three levels.

I do not intend the impossible, perhaps not even desirable, ideal that a husband and a wife should agree about everything on all three levels. I intend, rather, that each spouse must understand and come to terms with both his and her own needs, feelings, and desires on all three levels and also those of the other spouse, and that neither should use their married relationship for any end other than one in which the other is a full partner. All exclusive self-love, which is not at all the same thing as all self-love, for there is a legitimate self-love,[29] is excluded by a one-body relationship. For if spouses are to grow, individually and together, each needs both to esteem himself or herself and to feel esteemed by the other. Such oneness is not attained, of course, before, during or immediately after the wedding ceremony. It is learned only gradually as a husband and a wife discover, explore, and fulfill their separate and mutual possibilities on all three levels.

The universal, and far from just the modern, history of marriage demonstrates the difficulty of achieving such an intimate unity. It is constantly threatened by exclusive selfishness and the desire to control another human being. But it is a unity which must be achieved if a marriage is ever to become a one-body marriage. And until a marriage becomes a one-body marriage it is not an adequately representative symbol of the covenant union and love of Christ and his Church. At best it will remain an unconsummated marriage on any but the most superficial of levels, and only imperfectly sacramental. It is precisely because of the difficulties in becoming one body, and therefore adequately sacramental, that Christian marriage is an essentially eschatological symbol. That is, although it is already and inchoately prophetic symbol and sacrament of the covenant union between Christ and his Church, it is not yet the perfect symbol it needs to be. This already-but-not-yet dimension of Chrisitan marriage presents it with both a comfort and a challenge. A comfort to the extent that Christian spouses can claim, in faith and in truth, that their intimate union is both modeled upon and a model of the intimate union between Christ and his Church. A challenge to the extent that they confront constantly their falling short of and their need to be more attuned to their model.

Embodied Love

I must say a special word about the place of sexuality and sexual intercourse in a one-body Christian marriage, both because the Christian tradition has shown toward them an essential ambivalence and because many Christians have absorbed that ambivalence as an essential negativity. I believe it is foolish to pretend that there is no *theological* problem here; even our very brief conspectus of the history negates such a pretense. I believe it is equally foolish to say only that all the Christian need do about sexuality is to restrain its desires and to master them by self-denial. For, sadly, history again demonstrates that for many Christians, married and unmarried alike, unmitigated acceptance of their God-given gift of sexuality is a great deal more difficult than restraint. No, a special word needs to be said, and it must be a word of *reverse discrimination* to balance the negative message of the Western tradition with a more positive approach.

Some may judge that Tom Driver has said all there is to say. "Sex is not essentially human. It is not inseparable from the human in us, and it cannot be fully humanized. . . . Christianity should no more idealize sex than it should scorn or fear it."[30] But I feel I must demur. Driver is right if what he means is that sex is not *exclusively* human, but he is quite wrong if what he means is that it is not *essentially* human. He is also dead wrong when he says that sex is not inseparable from the human in us. Sexuality is, indeed, essentially human; there has never been a normal human being who was not sexual. Of course, we share sexuality with all animals, but that does not negate its essential humanness. We share all sorts of properties with other animals. Of course, we humans can use our sexuality only on the physical level of our being, and then it becomes detached from the human and is used only as animals use it. We can do that with any of our animal powers. But sexuality can be humanized; not by preempting it from the physical level (that cannot be done), but by letting it flow through all the three levels I have noted in the human, the physical, of course, but also the psychological and the spiritual. Sexuality, indeed, does not ever need to be humanized, for it is human to begin with. In a one-body marriage it can, indeed must, take on a distinctively and exclusively human form.

I wish to reemphasize here that one-body marriage requires a husband and a wife to become one on all three levels of their being, for I detect in modern Catholic theology a spiritualizing approach to sexuality and sexual intercourse in marriage. That approach locates the principal value of human sexuality and intercourse exclusively on the spiritual level. I share the same objection to such spiritualizing as that articulated by John Giles Milhaven, that it is not what the spiritualizing approach puts in but what it leaves out. "Man does do these spiritual, personal things in his sexual life (encounters, communicates, expresses love, etc.), and they do constitute the principal value of human sexuality, but not solely. The bodiliness and sexualness with which he does them changes intrinsically their nature and therefore their value from what they would be in a nonbodied, nonsexual person's life."[31] The encounter, the interpersonal communication, the love-making and every other spiritual interaction between a man and a woman are essentially embodied activities. There is no way to banish body from the human. To transfer human sexuality up to the exclusively spiritual level is just as untrue to human nature as is transferring it down to the exclusively animal level.

It is not difficult, however, to understand the mainspring of such a tactic. The elements of sexuality and of sexual intercourse that lie on the nonspiritual levels, especially those on the physical level, are precisely those dimensions that their tradition has so conditioned Christians to distrust. But I repeat, to become one body, and therefore sacrament of the covenant uniting Christ and his Church, Christian spouses must come to terms with their individual and mutual needs, feelings and desires on all three levels of being, including the distrusted physical. Becoming one person with another human being includes becoming not only one spirit and one mind, but also one body. Married love is *agape*, the love of the spouse for the spouse's sake, but it is also more than *agape*. Married love is *philia*, the love of the spouse as a friend, but it is also more than *philia*. Married love is *eros*, the love of the spouse for one's own sake, but it is also more than *eros*.

Married love that leads two to become one body is never exclusively selfish love, but it is unquestionably in part selfish love.

Now lest that smack of heresy in pious, unreflective ears, let me put it another way. Married love is loving your neighbor (spouse) *as yourself* (Matthew 22:39). Since Augustine, this great commandment has been recognized in the wisdom of the Catholic tradition as the basis for a wholly justifiable self-love. That justifiable self-love is very much evident when two persons have become one body. In such a marriage, each spouse is a full and fully esteemed partner and never just an object. In such a marriage, "I love you" grows truthfully into "I love me and you" or, as Milhaven puts it so beautifully, into "we love us."[32] One of the reasons that many Christian men and women have difficulty intimately loving another human person in marriage, even in Christian marriage, is that they have great difficulty in coming to love themselves.

And so to *eros*, that rambunctious, so-called impersonal, sub-human, and definitely selfish and nonrational component of human love and human sexuality. The spiritualizers always want to transform it into *agape*. But there is no alchemy to effect such a transformation; *eros* is an essential, and therefore inescapable, form of human love. We do better to accept it, to integrate it, and to give it a distinctively human form. That distinctive form appears, I believe, when the power of *eros* is harnessed by human wisdom. *Eros*, by definition, is the love of the spouse for one's own sake. Where *eros* dominates, I trample others and make them means to my ends. Such an approach produces what it seeks to avoid, emptiness and loneliness. Where wisdom dominates, I recognize that my partner's happiness is the only way that I, too, can be happy. In that wisdom, strangely, *eros* is not transformed into, but is allied to, *agape*. It is precisely this alliance of *eros* and *agape* that allows married love to persist and to grow when those things that fuel *eros*, youth, beauty, health, grace, have long since passed away.[33]

We may recall here that Augustine and Gregory judge *eros* negatively, that Aquinas hinted at its essential goodness, that Messenger transcended them all by asserting that the more heightened the passion and the pleasure the greater is the moral goodness in *eros*. That was a courageous and daring stroke against the Neo-Platonic tide that had swept the Western tradition along. But it is an argument that is sustained by the very tradition against which it moves, for that tradition holds that the more a created reality attains to its natural end, the truer and better and more moral it is. I prefer, though, to put the argument differently—and sacramentally. Sexuality, sexual passion, sexual pleasure, *eros*, derive their sacramental character, in the first instance, not from any purpose that human beings might assign to them, but from the simple theological fact that they are from God. They are God's gifts to *'adam* in his creation, and they are good gifts. To use them as good gifts of God in the process of becoming one in Christian marriage (and that is the only use I am considering in this discussion) is to use them in a way that points to their origin in God. That is already to use them sacramentally, in a way that is not only human, but also Christian and graceful.

But I agree with Messenger. The more heightened and sharply focused are sexual passion, sexual pleasure, *eros*, the more they achieve their very nature, the more the gift of God is valued, and the more the giver may be praised. And so in a genuine Christian marriage there is no need to fear them, no need to spiritualize them, no need to abstain from communion in the Body of Christ because of them. As I have said, for two human animals to become one body-person includes essentially, though not exclusively, becoming one body physically. This physically becoming one, even in its most passionately erotic form, is an element in the prophetic symbol of marriage, for it proclaims and makes real and celebrates in the symbol of his good gift the Giver who is himself gift and grace. Physical union, as ought to be clear from everything I have said, is not all there is to becoming one body. All I am doing here is underscoring that it has a place in Christian marriage, as prophetic symbol of the covenant uniting humanity and the God who does not shrink from proclaiming his love for his beloved in that most beautiful,and most erotic, of love songs, the Song of Songs.

The Song has always posed problems for both Jews and Christians, specifically the problem of whether it is a paean to divine or human love. For centuries, unwilling to consider that human, erotic love would have any place in the sacred Scriptures (and we have already dealt with the pagan sources of that unwillingness), commentators opted for an allegorical reading. The Song of Songs, they piously explained, was about divine love. But even if it is, God, good communicator that he is, always reveals himself in the language of his hearers. In the Song, where he reveals the depth and intensity of his love for his beloved Israel, he speaks in the extraordinarily explicit words of passionate erotic love. "I am sick with love," the young woman exclaims (2:5; 5:8). "Come to me," she cries out to her lover in desire, "like a gazelle, like a young stag upon the mountains where spices grow" (2:17; 8:14). When he comes, and gazes upon her naked, he is moved to ecstasy. "Your rounded thighs are like jewels, the work of a master hand. Your navel is a rounded bowl that never lacks mixed wine.[34] Your belly is a heap of wheat, encircled with lilies. Your two breasts are like two fawns, twins of a gazelle. Your neck is like an ivory tower. Your eyes are pools in Heshbon . . . Your nose is like a tower of Lebanon . . . Your head crowns you like Carmel, and your flowing locks are like purple; a king is held captive in the tresses. How fair and pleasant you are, loved one, delectable maiden. You are stately as a palm tree, and your breasts are like its clusters. I say I will climb the palm tree and lay hold of its branches" (7:1-8). Her reply is direct. "I am my beloved's, and his desire is for me. Come, my beloved, let us go forth into the fields, and lodge in the villages. Let us go out early to the vineyards . . . There I will give you my love" (7:10-12). No man or woman who has ever been sick with love can doubt the language or its intent.

Such explicitly erotic language has always caused commentators to doubt whether the Song is so evidently about divine love. But it was the emergence of the historical-critical approach to reading the Bible, since Pius XII the dominant approach in the Catholic tradition, that led to a growing consensus that the meaning of the Song was its literal meaning, and that that literal meaning was the meaning enshrined in any human love song. The Song may be an allegory about divine love, but only secondarily. It may be about "pure" love, in the sense of spiritual, nonerotic love, but only derivatively. It is directly about human, erotic love, about love that at least includes *eros*, about love that is joyfully sick with passion and desire. It is about the love of *'adam*, always male and female, who in love always seek the bodily presence of the other. This love is celebrated as gift, and therefore image, of the Creator God and of his love for *'adam*. It is celebrated, therefore, as good and worthy to be included in the biblical word to honor not only the giver, but also the gift and *'adam* who uses it to make not only human but also "divine" love.

In response to Driver's view that sex cannot be fully humanized, I say again that it does not need to be humanized because it is already fully human, precisely as gifted to *'adam* by the Creator-God. That human sexual passion can never be fully humanly mastered I grant, because such mastery attains only to the rational, and sexual passion and pleasure have much in them that is nonrational. But one fully human way to respond to the nonrational is to accept it joyfully and playfully. Man and woman, husband and wife, do not become fully human by ignoring *eros*, or by negotiating their way carefully around it, above it or beyond it. They become human only by accepting it and integrating it into the rest of their human—and Christian—lives.

And so, in summary, what can we say of marriage? We can say that *secular* marriage is a God-gifted, life-long community of love to ensure the most appropriate conditions for life, the life of the spouses with one another as couple and with any children as family.[35] *Christian* marriage is that very same secular marriage perceived and lived in faith as prophetic symbol and sacrament of the community of love resulting from the covenant between Christ and his Church.

The Minister of Christian Marriage

It has been the traditional teaching of the Western Church that the two people marrying *minister* the sacrament of marriage one to the other. The identification of marriage contract and marriage sacrament made that conclusion inescapable. There is still, of course, a sense in which that is true. To the extent that the couple still mutually covenant and that the marriage covenant between faithful is identical with the sacrament, a believing couple minister the sacrament to one another. But, if what I have argued about the specificity of Christian marriage over any other marriage is correct, then a more nuanced answer to the question of minister is required. I shall argue that the law, still in force (CIC,1983, Canon 1108), which requires for the validity of a Christian marriage the presence of a priest or deacon, is a law requiring the presence of more than a legal witness to the couple's covenant. For the priest or deacon receives their mutual covenant "in the name of the church" (Canon 1108).

In secular marriage a man and a woman consent to bind themselves one to the other. In Christian marriage they do that—and more. They bind themselves to live and to love not only as spouses but also as *Christian* spouses, as domestic Church. They bind themselves, that is, to reveal and to make real and to celebrate in and through their

marriage not only their covenant and community but also the covenant and community between Christ and his Church. That Church,
which they are to be in microcosm, has a stake in their marriage. Since
its covenant with its Christ is to be represented in and through the
prophetic symbol of this marriage, it needs to know whether this
couple can offer an adequate Christian representation of its covenant
with Christ and it needs to prepare them to do so. Hence, in some kind
of Pre-Marriage Inventory, it inquires into their talent not just for
marriage, but specifically for Christian marriage. The presence of its
designated minister at a marriage announces that in the case of this
particular couple that talent has been found to be present.

The Church's minister is present, therefore, at a Christian
marriage to be more than just a simple witness to their giving and
receiving of consent. If that was all there was to it, then all marriages of
the faithful would not require a designated witness at all. No, the
ordained minister is present to perform certain functions in the name
of the Church. He is there to attest to the faith of this couple as the
faith of the Church. He is there to attest also to the talent-charism this
couple possesses, not only for marriage but specifically for Christian
marriage. He is there to receive the couple's consent, to live not only in
irrevocable love for one another but also in irrevocable representation
of the union between Christ and his Church. He is there to commission
the couple in the name of that Church to be in their married Christian
life the prophetic symbol of this union. He is there, finally, to bless
them in the name of the Church (and therefore in the name of Christ
and of God), and to promise them the support of the Church in their
given and accepted task. The position which views the minister of the
sacrament of marriage as *exclusively* the couple misses these ecclesial
dimensions, and risks communicating the message that Christian
marriage is just a private matter between this couple. The reality is
that, however much merely secular marriage may be a private matter
between a man and a woman, Christian marriage is not. It is, of
course, a private matter for the couple. But it is also a public matter for
the Church, and the Church's ordained representative is required to be
present to take care of the Church's legitimate concerns in the matter.

While I do not believe that we need to go all the way to the
position of the Eastern Church, which views the priest as the sole
minister of the sacrament of marriage, I do believe that we need to go
beyond the established Western position, which sees the priest or

deacon as merely a legal witness. We need to see him as a *co-minister* of the sacrament of Christian marriage. Such a development, I believe, is legitimate. It is also necessary to proclaim that Christian marriage is not just a private matter for the intended spouses, but is also a public matter for the entire Church, whose covenant with Christ they are to symbolize in their marriage. That proclamation, it seems to me, needs very much to be heard, especially in the Western world. For there, in contrast to other cultures in which society's stake in marriage is so well acknowledged that marriages are arranged by other than the intended spouses, there is a strong emphasis on individualism and free choice. In such a climate it needs to be emphasized that in a Christian marriage the Christian Church has as much stake in the marriage as the individuals marrying. The minister of the Church is present at a Christian marriage both to proclaim and to protect, in symbol, that stake.

Summary

This chapter sought to be about a contemporary Roman Catholic theology of Christian marriage. It sought to clarify, first, the distinction between marriage as a universal secular reality and marriage as a specifically Christian sacrament. That distinction is found in an added dimension possessed by Christian marriage, a dimension which transforms the universal reality of secular marriage into a specifically prophetic symbol of the union existing between Christ and his Church. It sought to oppose the *Code of Canon Law* by establishing that there is no automatic sacrament of Christian marriage just because two baptized Christians mutually consent to be married. All sacraments, including the sacrament of marriage, are sacraments of faith. Only the active Christian faith of the marrying persons actively embracing that added prophetic dimension found in Christian marriage transforms valid secular marriage into grace-full Christian sacrament. Without such transforming faith two people can, of course, enter into a valid secular marriage, but they cannot enter into a valid Christian sacrament. This crucial point makes it clear that the new *Code of Canon Law* must be judged to be at best a transitional statement between a medieval and juridical theology of sacrament and marriage which excluded too many things and a contemporary and interpersonal theology which includes more things than the *Code* has yet covered.

This chapter also sought to set in clear relief a threefold reality found in the human animal, physical, psychological, and spiritual, and to integrate all three levels in the quest to become one body-person. A special note of emphasis was laid on erotic love and its place in a Christian marriage, not because such love is the be-all and end-all of a marriage, but only because the Christian tradition has been largely negative towards such love and its rightful place in Christian marriage.

Finally, this chapter sought to demonstrate that Christian marrige is not only a private matter for the entire Church, whose covenant with Christ is to be symboled prophetically in it. On the basis of this ecclesial character of Christian marriage it is argued that the minister, whose presence is required for the validity of the marriage since the Council of Trent, is more than just a legal witness. He is also a co-minister with believing Christians of religious sacrament.

Questions for Reflection and Discussion

1. Do you believe that everyone who is baptized really attains to Christian faith? Or are there baptized nonbelievers in your community?

2. If the Roman Catholic Church teaches, on the one hand, that a sacrament cannot be effective without some minimal contribution of Christian faith on the part of the participant, does it make any sense to claim, on the other hand, that two people enter into a sacramental marriage just because they have been baptized? Explain.

3. Or is it enough just to be married in church before a priest and two witnesses in order to enter into a sacramental marriage?

4. How do you feel about your sexuality and its use in marriage as a source of grace and holiness? (This is one of the things the Roman Catholic Church means when it says that Christian marriage is a sacrament.)

5. Are you comfortable or uncomfortable with the claim that Christian marriage is a matter for the whole Church and not just for the marrying couple? Why? Does it make more sense to you to say that the priest is merely a witness of marriage or to say that he is also a co-minister of it with the couple?

Divorce and Remarriage: Theory and Practice in the Catholic Church

The Scriptures of the Old Testament hold up to us the extreme fidelity of Hosea in his marriage despite every provocation from his faithless wife. They offer us also the exhortation of the later prophet, Malachi, to hate divorce, at least, as we saw in the opening chapter, divorce between Jew and Jew. That demand to be faithful and to hate divorce becomes the Christian gospel, the message and the challenge to one who claims to be a follower of Jesus the Christ. The gospels report four times that Jesus delivered a judgment against divorce and remarriage: in Matthew 5:32 and 19:9, in Luke 16:18, and in Mark 10:11–12. Paul, who writes well before any of the gospel writers, also reports a prohibition of divorce and remarriage, and attributes it to the Lord (1 Corinthians 7:10–11). That gospel message becomes the well-known, if not well-understood, law of the Catholic Church, namely that Christian marriage is indissoluble. It is precisely because both the gospel and the law that flows from it are not well-understood that I plan to reflect on this question at length. My hope is that such reflection will be of help, not only to those Catholics who are married, but also to those others who have been married and are now separated or divorced or remarried, in understanding their marriage situation in the eyes of their Church.

In the public understanding the matter would appear to be simple and straightforward: the Roman Catholic Church does not allow divorce. But in Church theory and practice, the matter is far from that simple and straightforward. It appears useful to me, therefore, to cut through the confusion at the outset by setting forth that long-established theory and practice, and then moving toward its explanation and understanding. The 1983 *Code of Canon Law,* which is the present culmination of centuries of theory and practice, states that theory and practice succinctly.

Canon 1141 states what kind of marriage cannot be dissolved by anyone. "A marriage which is ratified and consummated cannot be dissolved by any human power or by any cause other than death." There it is, almost as clear as crystal. The Catholic Church forbids divorce in the case of a ratified and consummated marriage. I say "almost as clear as crystal," for the term *ratified* in the Canon is not as clear as it needs to be, for what it really intends is much more precise than what it actually says. It intends "a marriage which is ratified and consummated *as sacrament."* Now, there is the teaching and the law of the Roman Catholic Church as clear as crystal. Only that marriage which is ratified and consummated as Christian sacrament is held to be indissoluble. Marriages between baptized persons which are not consummated are dissoluble, and are dissolved by the pope for a just reason (Canon 1142). Marriages between nonbaptized persons, which are therefore nonsacramental, are dissoluble and are dissolved by the pope *in favorem fidei,* in favor of the faith (Canon 1143). I hope it is clear that the public understanding of the question discussed above is very simplistic, and needs to be refined. That the Roman Catholic Church forbids divorce is not entirely correct. That it forbids the dissolution by anyone, including the Roman Pontiff, of a marriage which is ratified and consummated as Christian sacrament, that is correct. That it forbids the dissolution by any merely human authority of any kind of valid marriage, that is correct; and therefore it does not accept as valid any dissolution of a marriage by a civil court. But that it forbids the dissolution under every circumstance of any valid marriage, even by the Bishop of Rome, that is quite incorrect. The rest of this chapter will be devoted to the explanation and understanding of these refinements.

Divorce and Remarriage in the New Testament

As I have already stated, the Synoptic Gospels record words of Jesus about divorce and remarriage four times: in Mark 10:11-12, in Matthew 5:32 and 19:9, and in Luke 16:18. Paul, in 1 Corinthians 7:10-11, reports a prohibition of divorce and remarriage and attributes it to the Lord. To understand these New Testament passages to the fullest, we must understand two things: first, the nature of the gospel writings and, secondly, the traditional Jewish context of the sayings about divorce and remarriage. Before seeking to understand the New Testament sayings about divorce and remarriage, we must seek first to understand these background matters.

First, then, the nature of the gospels. On two different occasions in 1964, the Roman Catholic Church sought to give its definitive answer to the question: what kind of writings are the gospels? In April of that year, in an *Instruction on the Historical Truth of the Gospels*, the Pontifical Biblical Commission warned that "in order to determine correctly the trustworthiness of what is transmitted in the gospels, the interpreter must take careful note of the three stages of tradition by which the teaching and the life of Jesus have come down to us."[1] In November of the same year, in its *Dogmatic Constitution on Divine Revelation*, the Second Vatican Council made it clear that this three-stage approach was the official Roman Catholic position on the truth of the gospels. It taught that "the sacred authors wrote the four gospels, selecting some things from the many which had been handed on by word of mouth or in writing, reducing some of them to a synthesis, explicating some things in view of the situation of their churches, and preserving the form of proclamation but always in such fashion that they told the honest truth about Jesus."[2]

What do we have, therefore, in the gospels? Or, perhaps better and more to the point for a modern reader, what do we not have? We do not have a detailed biography of all that Jesus said and did, as John himself openly tells us. "Jesus did many other signs in the presence of the disciples, which are not written in this book. But these are written that you may believe that Jesus is the Christ, the Son of God" (20:30–31).

So what do we have? We can state the historical sequence of what we have somewhat like this. In a first stage, we have what Jesus of Nazareth said and did, roughly between the years 4 B.C.E. and 30 C.E.. In a second stage, following the death of Jesus, there develop, roughly between the years 30 and 65, traditions about what Jesus said and did and meant. In a third stage, the gospel *authors,* not *secretaries,* roughly between the years 65 and 90, sift through this traditional material, selecting from it what addressed the needs of their churches and writing their selections in a literary context. Those are the three historical stages by which the gospels came into existence. They yield three strata in the gospels as we have them: a stratum in which we find what Jesus said and did, a stratum in which we find what the traditions said that Jesus said and did and meant, and a stratum in which we find what the gospel authors wrote of it all in light of the situation of their churches. We shall have to keep in mind that it is the third stratum that is most easily accessible to us when we read the gospels today and, also, the time lapse between the first and the third stages. Jesus died about the year 30, and the first gospel by Mark did not appear until the late 60s; Matthew and Luke followed in the 80s, and John about 90. We shall see what all this means when we consider the New Testament divorce statements.

The gospel writers situate the sayings of Jesus about divorce and remarriage in the context of some Jewish presuppositions. To understand Jesus' sayings fully we need to consider those presuppositions. We need to know what Jews of the time of Jesus meant by both marriage and divorce. In Jesus' world marriage was a family affair in the sense that families married. "In the first-century Mediterranean world and earlier, marriage symbolizes the fusion of the honor of two extended families and is undertaken with a view to political and/or economic concerns."[3] Males draw up a marriage contract, which includes bridewealth for the father of the bride, and eventually the father surrenders his daughter to the groom who takes her as his wife by bringing her into his own house. This process results in the disembedding of a daughter from the honor of her father and her embedding as wife in the honor of her new husband. It creates between husband and wife a bond that is not a legal bond, as it is in contemporary Western society, but a sort of blood relationship which is called a "one body" relationship. In the marriage a wife does not look to her husband for affection or companionship or comfort. She looks to him to be a good provider and an honorable citizen. Divorce was the reversal of this marriage process. "Divorce means the process of disembedding the female from the honor of the male, along with a sort of redistribution and return of the honor of the families concerned."[4] Divorce, like marriage, was a family affair.

The differences we need to note between both marriage and divorce in the time of Jesus and in our own time are clear. In modern Western society, neither marriage nor divorce is a family affair in the sense just described. They are rather individual affairs. A man and a woman marry, for love we say, seeking from one another interpersonal affection, companionship, support and comfort. They marry with or without the approval of their respective families. Their marriage creates between them not a blood bond, but a legal one. When they seek a divorce, therefore, they do not presume that they themselves can dissolve the marriage, but they petition the proper legal authority to do so. In the divorce proceedings, which either one may initiate, their concerns are never about extended family and honor, but about economics and property (including children). All of this reveals quite different presuppositions from those held in Jesus' day, not only among Jews but also among Romans. In Roman law, the spouses themselves dissolved their marriage, simply by withdrawing their will to be married. Just as their will to be married had married them, so also their will to be unmarried unmarried them. In Jewish law it was quite different. Only the husband could dissolve the marriage, and he did so simply by writing his wife a bill of divorce and dismissing her, a practice which was prescribed in Torah.

In the Book of Deuteronomy we read, "When a man takes a wife and marries her, if then she finds no favor in his eyes because he has found some indecency (*erwat dabar*) in her, and he writes her a bill of divorce and puts it in her hand and sends her out of his house, and she departs from his house, and if she goes and becomes another man's wife . . . then her former husband who sent her away may not take her again to be his wife, after she has been defiled" (24:1–4). In this passage we find the right of the husband to divorce his wife, the prohibition to remarry a spouse he has divorced and the ground for divorce. The ground is "something indecent," *erwat dabar*, a very general ground which could only provoke dispute over its interpretation. In the generation prior to Jesus that dispute had split into two camps, one following the great Rabbi Hillel, the other following the great Rabbi Shammai. Hillel and his disciples interpreted *erwat dabar* broadly. It intended some serious moral, sexual delinquency, but it intended also delinquency other than moral. Shammai and his school interpreted *erwat dabar* strictly. It intended only serious moral, sexual delinquency. The great debate continued to rage at the time of Jesus, and we shall see how it provides the context for Jesus' sayings about divorce in the gospels.

As already indicated, Mark is the first of the gospel writers, writing some thirty-seven years after the death of Jesus. He writes, so tradition holds, for a Roman Christian community, which we shall have to bear in mind if we are to understand the three strata in the passage under review. That passage is in 10:2–12. "Pharisees came up and *in order to test him* asked, 'Is it lawful for a man to dismiss (*apolusai*) his wife?' He answered them, 'What did Moses *command* you?' They said, 'Moses *permitted* a man to write a certificate of divorce, and to dismiss her.' But Jesus said to them, 'For your hardness of heart he wrote you this *commandment*. But *from the beginning* of creation God made them male and female. For this reason a man shall leave his father and mother and be joined to his wife, and the two shall become one flesh. So they are no longer two but one flesh. What therefore God has joined together, let not man put asunder.' And in the house the disciples asked him again about this matter. And he said to them, 'Whoever dismisses his wife and marries another commits adultery against her. And if she dismisses her husband and marries another, she commits adultery.' "

The last sentence tells us the audience for which Mark was writing. It tells us also that it is probably not a saying of Jesus, but an interpolation by Mark. That a wife would dismiss her husband is simply unheard of in the Palestinian Judaism of Jesus' day, and therefore it would make no sense for Jesus to say something like that. It is, of course, a possibility in Roman Law, and Mark has no qualms about interpreting the words of Jesus in light of the needs of his Roman Church. The author also presents the divorce tradition in the context of a dispute with the Pharisees. Now whether this context is from the historical life of Jesus, or from the life of Mark and his community, we have no way of knowing for sure. Ultimately, it does not matter, for in either case it is accepted as gospel by the Catholic Church.

The Pharisees set out, yet again (see also Mark 8:11 and 12:13), to test Jesus. This time they seek to test his honor and his allegiance in the dispute between Hillel and Shammai. Hence their question: "Is it lawful for a man to dismiss his wife?" Jesus replies with a question: "What did Moses *command* you?" Their reply refuses to acknowledge a command from Moses, but only a permission. But Jesus insists on the command nature of the Torah injunction, a command given because of their unfaithfulness, their hardness of heart, a command that was "not good" but which was given, as Ezekiel reports, "that they might know that I am Yahweh" (20:25–26). He insists that it was not so "from the beginning of creation," insinuating that Moses' commandment and their interpretation of it is an innovation which is counter to Yahweh's will in the beginning. Pushing the discussion beyond Moses to the beginning brings into play everything that is in the Genesis story about male and female; bone of bone and flesh of flesh; a man leaving his father and his mother to cleave to his wife, to become with her one body. We saw in the opening chapter of this work that that "one body" means much more than just sexual union, though it implies and includes such union. It means, ultimately, one person.

Jesus' argument against the Pharisees is that God's will from the beginning was that a man and a woman are so joined in marriage that before God, and therefore before the people, they are one person. How, then, could a man dismiss this one person, his very own person, in divorce? We saw earlier the very same kind of argument made by the author of the letter to the Ephesians: "Husbands should love their wives as their own bodies; he who loves his wife loves himself" (5:28). Jesus' conclusion, and his teaching as articulated by Mark, is that marriage as intended by God in the beginning is indissoluble. "What therefore God has joined together, let not man put asunder," not even a Jewish man claiming to follow Torah. And, in the literarily contrived conversation "in the house," Mark articulates in a parable saying what it all means for the disciples of Jesus, in Jesus' day, in Mark's day and in our day. "Whoever divorces his wife and marries another commits adultery against her." For the sake of his Roman audience, Mark extends that to the case, unheard of in Jewish law, but perfectly possible in Roman law, of the wife dismissing her husband.

Matthew has two versions of Jesus's sayings on divorce, a short one and a long one. The short one is located within the Sermon on the Mount. "It was also said, 'Whoever divorces his wife, let him give her a certificate of divorce.' But I say to you that everyone who divorces his wife, except on the ground of *porneia*, makes her an adulteress; and whoever marries a divorced woman commits adultery" (5:31–32). The long one is situated in the context of a dispute between Jesus and the Pharisees, who seek to put him to the test. In outline it is very similar to Mark's version, probably because Matthew borrowed it from Mark, but there are significant differences of detail.

The test to which Jesus is submitted in Matthew is again a test of whether he sides with Hillel or Shammai in the great debate about *erwat dabar*, or *porneia*, as the Septaugint version chose to translate it. The Pharisees ask him: "Is it lawful to divorce one's wife for *any cause?*" (19:3). A positive answer would have placed Jesus on the side of Hillel's broad interpretation; a negative answer would have placed him on the side of Shammai's restrictive one. We can surmise that the test this time was designed to cause Jesus to lose the adherents of whichever side he did not choose. But, as in Mark, though this time more quickly, Jesus refuses the terms of the question, and returns the discussion to "the beginning" (19:4) chronicled in Genesis, in which it "was not so" (19:8). His teaching is the same as in Mark: "They are no longer two but one body. What therefore God has joined together, let not man put asunder" (19:6). And so, as in Mark, though with a significant addition, there is the ultimate conclusion. "Whoever divorces his wife, except for *porneia*, and marries another, commits adultery. And he who marries a divorced woman commits adultery" (19:9). Jesus' response to the test is to refuse to side with either Hillel or Shammai and to return the discussion to a more radical question than the legitimate cause for divorce. He seeks to have them ask whether divorce is possible at all, and answers negatively, because such is what an authority greater than Moses, namely, Yahweh, intended in the beginning.

Jesus' position and his teaching about divorce and remarriage would have been indisputably clear were it not for that exceptive phrase, *epi tes porneia*, except for *porneia*, found in both of Matthew's versions and not in Mark's or Luke's. The meaning of that phrase, as can be expected, has been endlessly disputed, just as Jews of Jesus' time disputed the meaning of *erwat dabar*. I have no intention of entering into that dispute in this book, since I am persuaded that we cannot know now the meaning of the phrase in Matthew's intent.[5] I wish to raise here quite a different question: does the exceptive clause originate in the teaching of Jesus or in the authorship of Matthew? Is it from that stratum of the gospel which faithfully records the words and deeds of Jesus, or is it from that stratum which derives from the author in the light of the needs of his Christian community? I agree with the majority scholarly opinion that the latter is the case, given Matthew's established penchant for adding to the words of Jesus for his own designs, and given the absence of the phrase in Mark, Luke, and Paul. I wish to underscore only one conclusion from that. Being fully aware of Jesus' position on divorce and remarriage, Matthew still did not hesitate to make an addition to that position in the light of the needs of his church. That church, all are agreed, was a Jewish-Christian church, that is, one composed of Jews who had been "converted" to Christianity, but who still adhered to the Jewish law. Paul, too, did not hesitate to contribute his interpretation.

In chapter seven of his First Letter to the Corinthians, written long before any of the gospels, perhaps as early as the year 52, Paul provides answers to questions posed to him by the Corinthian community. That community was a mixed Jewish-Hellenistic community, which explains Paul's choice of words for his instruction on divorce. Sometimes he has Jewish law in mind, in which only the husband has the power to dismiss the wife; sometimes he has the Roman law in mind, in which both husband and wife have the power to dismiss the other. In apparent response to a question about divorce Paul offers a command, which he claims is from the Lord. "To the married I give charge, not I but the Lord, that a wife is not to be separated (*choristhenai*) from her husband. And if she is separated, she is to remain unmarried or is to be reconciled to her husband. And a husband is not to dismiss (*aphienai*) his wife (7:10–11).

The custom of divorce was deeply rooted in the traditions that the Corinthians knew, and it is not difficult to imagine them wishing to know what they were supposed to do about it as Christians. Paul leaves them in no doubt what should be their attitude as Christians: "the wife is not to be separated from her husband," nor is the husband to dismiss his wife. It would appear, from the verbs he uses, that Paul has in mind the divorce custom common to Jewish and Roman law, that is, the dismissal of the wife by the husband. The husband is not to *dismiss* his wife, and the wife is "not *to be separated*" (that is, by someone else) from her husband. But if he had in mind the Roman law, as well as the Rabbinic one, then why did he not add, as did Mark, the phrase forbidding the wife to dismiss the husband? And why does he specify, in the case in which a wife has been separated from her Christian husband (does that mean that in Christian Corinth divorce was practiced?), only what the wife must do then, making no mention of what the husband should do? There is some problem about getting at the precise details of Paul's instruction to Christian spouses about divorce. But that problem does not reach to the matter in question here, what is to be the attitude of Corinthian Christians to divorce and remarriage. That attitude seems to be clear: a marriage between Christians is not to be dissolved by the wife's dismissal, that is, in the Jewish way. We might wish to extend that prohibition to include the husband's dismissal in the Roman way (though Paul says nothing about it here), and conclude in general that the dissolution of a marriage between Christians is forbidden (which is not the same thing as saying that it is intrinsically impossible).

Having dealt with the question of divorce in the case of the marriage of two Christians, Paul then proceeds to the discussion of a case of conscience about divorce that must have been very prevalent in the earliest Christian communities, just as it is very prevalent in mission communities today. As we shall see, the solution Paul gave there is the very same solution that the Catholic Church gives now. The case is this: what about divorce in the marriage in which one spouse has become Christian and the other has remained non-Christian? Paul has two pieces of advice for the spouses in such marriages, each of them hinging on the attitude of the non-Christian spouse.

The first advice covers the case in which the non-Christian partner is perfectly willing to continue to live with the Christian spouse. In this case, "if any brother has a wife who is an unbeliever, and she consents to live with him, he should not dismiss her. If any woman has a husband who is an unbeliever, and he consents to live with her, she should not dismiss him" (7:12–13). It would appear that Paul is now thinking firmly within the context of Roman law, in which both husband and wife have the right to end the marriage by dismissing the other. And his instruction is firm: when the unbelieving spouse is willing to live in marriage with the believer, he or she is not to be dismissed. The Genesis epigrammatic instruction stands firm: what God has joined together, let not man put asunder.

Just as it did in the time of Ezra and Nehemiah and Malachi, however, as we saw in the opening chapter, that teaching comes under interpretation and exception in Paul's second advice. What of the case in which the unbeliever is unwilling to continue to live in marriage with the believer? "But if the unbelieving spouse desires to separate (*chorizetai*), let him separate; the brother or sister is not to play the slave (*dedoulotai*) in such matters" (7:15). Notice the verb. It is separate, *chorizetai*, a verb which indicates an action which the agent does. It is the unbeliever who separates himself or herself; he is not separated, or dismissed, by the believing spouse. There is no suggestion that the marriage of the believer and the unbeliever is not a valid marriage. There is no suggestion that Jesus' remembered instruction does not apply in this case. There is only the suggestion that in this case Paul is making an exception ("I say, not the Lord," (7:12). And the sole reason he gives for the exception is "the brother or sister is not to play the slave in such matters. For God has called us to peace" (7:15). It is an interesting reason.

In this second scenario, the attempt of the Christian spouse to hold the non-Christian spouse to the marriage, the attempt to bring him or her back to the marriage, to seek the reconciliation Paul has recommended above for Christian spouses (7:11), would simply destroy the peace to which a Christian is called by God. It is, as I have said, an interesting reason for an exception to Jesus' well-remembered instruction, in America today as in Corinth in 52. Peace, it seems, is a greater value than preserving a valid marriage. The Roman Catholic Church sanctioned this reason and this approach to dissolving a valid marriage in the twelfth century, still sanctions hem today, and names the process the Pauline Privilege. I shall deal with that privilege in its proper place.

We are now in a position to reflect on the New Testament teaching on divorce and remarriage. Our first reflection must be that it is not at all correct to speak of the New Testament *teaching*, for there are several *teachings*, and they are not in agreement. Nor are they all derived solely from Jesus, as is frequently and simplistically claimed and put forward as the reason why the Roman Catholic must continue to be opposed to divorce and remarriage.

There is a well-remembered saying of Jesus which scholars agree was probably originally that reported in Luke 16:18: "Everyone who divorces his wife and marries another commits adultery." In Luke's reaction the saying is an isolated one. But in both Mark and Matthew it is located in a careful literary setting to highlight not only its importance but also its difficulty. Mark (10:2–12) offers the saying at the conclusion of a "discussion" with the Pharisees, though Jesus does not make the statement before the Pharisees but before his disciples when he is alone with them later. "Now such a setting for a saying is quite familiar in Mark. It is the ordinary trapping of mystery (cf. Mark 6:10,37; 7:17; 9:33 etc.)."[6] Matthew (19:3–12) also presents the saying in the context of a dispute with the Pharisees. But he has Jesus state it in the public disputation and then explain it later to the disciples. This is his standard way of presenting particularly difficult material. The explanation of the saying is the parable of the eunuchs: " . . . there are eunuchs who have been so from birth, and there are eunuchs who have been made so by men, and there are eunuchs who have made themselves eunuchs for the sake of the kingdom of heaven" (19:12). What clarification does the eunuch parable bring to Jesus' traditional saying about divorce? Only that it is a saying not about divorce but about remarriage.

The prevailing Jewish tradition about a marriage in which there was *erwat dabar* or *porneia* was that a husband had to divorce his wife and could not remarry her. The eunuch parable clarifies Jesus' saying about divorce, as reported by Matthew with his exceptive clause, by explaining that though a husband could divorce his wife if there was *porneia*, he could not remarry her or anyone else. Matthew knows this is a hard saying. That is the very point of the objection made by the disciples: "If such is the case of a man with his wife, it is not expedient to marry" (19:10). Many of the sayings of Jesus that Matthew reports are hard, sayings about plucking out your eye (5:29), about cutting off your hand (5:30), about selling your goods and giving the proceeds to the poor (8:21), about losing your life to find it (10:39), about taking up your cross (16:24). But neither Jesus nor Matthew backs off the saying. Rather he reinforces it, explaining that it is not a demand made of everyone but only of those who would be his disciples. "He who is able to receive this," therefore, "let him receive it" (19:12).

Jesus is reported as saying: "Every one who divorces his wife and marries another commits adultery." Malina argues that "if this is what Jesus said, it has to be a parable." For "when taken literally, it makes as little sense as 'you are the salt of the earth' or 'you are the light of the world,'" and "in the Gospels of Matthew and Mark this teaching requires further, private explanation, a procedure these authors use for parables."[7] If it is a parable, it requires further interpretation for the concrete circumstances in which its hearers find themselves. That concrete interpretation is exactly what the New Testament writers provide.

Mark adds something that Jesus could never have said in his context, for it would have made no sense. That addition prohibits a wife to dismiss her husband (Mark 10:12). Matthew, good Jew that he is, adds his exceptive clause, except for *porneia*, whatever it might have meant in his mind. Paul adds his own genuine exception, covering the case of a marriage in which an unbelieving spouse wishes no longer to live with a believing one. Whatever personal preference anyone might have, I believe that Mackin's judgment cannot be gainsayed. "Because every element of the instruction on divorce and remarriage is part of the Gospel (and this includes the instruction in 1 Corinthians, even that part coming from Paul himself), it would falsify our reading of this Gospel if we were to single out one element, play it off against the others and make it override them."[8] Such a ploy would, indeed, falsify the New Testament tradition so sacred to Christians. Diverging accounts of the question of divorce and remarriage, as of many other crucial things, are an integral part of that tradition. There are diverging accounts, we now believe, because divergent Christian communities had divergent pressing concerns that needed to be answered. That is what Mark did, and Matthew and Paul. That the popular wisdom in the Catholic stream of the later Western tradition singled out one element in those diverging accounts, namely, the element of the indissolubility of a marriage, and allowed that element to override all the others ought never be allowed to obscure the original divergence.

I believe I can conclude this section by reciting the words of Vatican II I cited earlier, for I believe that now they will be more intelligible. "The sacred authors wrote the four gospels, selecting some things from the many which had been handed on by word of mouth or in writing, reducing some of them to a synthesis, explicating some things in view of the situation of their churches, and preserving the form of proclamation, but always in such fashion that *they told the honest truth about Jesus.*" So did the sacred authors in the instructions on divorce and remarriage. They selected, reduced, added and still told us the honest truth about Jesus. That honest truth would appear to be that Jesus taught that the one-body marriage, willed by God from the beginning, constitutes a man and a woman in such an interpersonal unity that every human authority is *forbidden* to dissolve it. I say forbidden to dissolve it, and not powerless to dissolve it, because probably Matthew and certainly Paul did not believe that that is what Jesus intended. Believing this, they formulated their own version of the aphorism: What God has joined together let not man put asunder—except in the case of . . . The Roman Catholic Church, as we shall see, has followed their formulation for centuries, and continues to follow it today.

The Development of the New Testament Teaching in the Church

In the first three centuries of the existence of the Christian church, Jesus' saying about divorce and remarriage, at least as it was understood, was reinforced. Included in the understanding of Jesus' teaching was the exceptive clause in Matthew, which was taken to be the word of Jesus himself. But there were uncertainties about interpretation, both in theory and in practice. In a book composed, as the Muratorian canon says, "in the city of Rome, by Hermas, while his brother Pius was sitting on the throne of the church of the city of Rome," between the years 140 and 154, we learn something of interest. The book, known as *The Shepherd of Hermas*, is divided into a series of visions, mandates, and parables. In Mandate IV we find a conversation between Hermas and his shepherd, the Angel of Penitence, relating to the question of divorce and remarriage.

Hermas asks, "If a man has a wife who believes in the Lord and he surprises her in adultery, does he commit a sin if he lives with her?" The angel's reply is two-pronged. If he does not know of her sin, then he does not sin in living with her. "But, if her husband knows the sin, and she does not repent but persists in her fornication, he becomes guilty of her sin as long as he lives with her." Hermas asks then, what is a husband to do in this latter case? "Let him dismiss her and remain single. But if he dismisses her and marries another woman, he himself commits adultery." The adulterous wife must be dismissed for adultery, but the husband must remain unmarried, "to bring about her repentance," as the angel goes on to explain.[9] This teaching provides a good summary of the ethic of the early Church. A spouse, at least a wife, must be dismissed for adultery. Such dismissal, though, in contrast to the established practice of Roman law, does not constitute a dissolution of the marriage, but merely a separation. Neither spouse, therefore, is free to remarry. As in Judaism a husband must divorce a wife guilty of adultery; unlike Judaism he may remarry her if she repents and they are reconciled.

On the other hand, there is Tertullian, certainly a legitimate representative of the teaching of the Latin Church (at least before he became a Montanist). Tertullian provides us with information so confusing that it can serve as paradigm for the confusion in the early Western Church. At the opening of his second book, *To a Wife*, he recalls to his wife how he had exhorted her in the first book to remain unmarried after his death, for absolute monogamy was God's will. Then he turns to the example of some Christian women who did not follow that advice, but remarried. "Having been offered, either by divorce (*divortio*) or the deaths of their husbands, the opportunity to live lives of continence, they not only rejected the opportunity for so great a good, but also in marrying again they did not even deign to remember the discipline that they marry in the Lord."[10] Tertullian berates these women for passing up the opportunity to live a virtuous life of continence and especially for marrying non-Christians. But, and this is of supreme interest to us in this chapter, he does not condemn them for remarrying after divorce. That he truly means divorce is quite clear from his choice of the normal word for it, *divortium*.

Tertullian returns briefly to the question of divorce a little further on, in the context of Paul's teaching in Corinthians about the marriage of a Christian and a pagan. He asks why the Christian spouse is not permitted to divorce the pagan partner, or let him or her depart, and answers that in this Pauline teaching the Lord is giving the instruction that such a marriage is not to be contracted, rather than that it is to be dissolved. But, in the end, the Lord "forbids divorce, except in the case of unchastity (*nisi stupri causa*)."[11] Certain things seem clear about Tertullian's teaching at this Catholic point of his life. First, divorce is permitted to Christians but exclusively on the ground of unchastity of the other spouse. Secondly, remarriage is permitted to Christians, though he prefers the second marriage to be to another Christian, and prefers above all perpetual continence. Later on in his life, during his Montanist period, though he will condemn any second marriage, Tertullian will continue to be quite confused, and indeed contradictory, about the question of Christians and divorce.

The fourth century was a time of great development in both doctrine and discipline in both the Eastern and the Western Christian Churches. The doctrine and the discipline with respect to divorce and remarriage were no exception to this judgment. In the East, two great bishops, Basil of Caesarea and John Chrysostom of Constantinople, created and lastingly shaped the marriage doctrine and discipline of the Eastern Churches. Two great Fathers, Jerome and especially Augustine, did the same for the Western Church. Therefore, we must consider the teachings of these men.

Basil deals with separation and remarriage in Rule 73 of his *Moralia*. Appealing predictably to Matthew 5:31–32, he prescribes that "a husband should not separate from his wife, nor a wife from her husband, unless the other spouse be taken in adultery or be an obstacle to piety." Matthew's exceptive clause, taken at the time to be a saying of the Lord's, is accepted without demur as a legitimate cause for separation. Indeed, throughout the East the adultery of one spouse imposed upon the other the *obligation* to separate from him or her. But after such separation could either spouse remarry? In the *Moralia*, Basil replies no. "It is not permitted to a husband who has dismissed his wife to marry another. Nor is it permitted to a wife who has been repudiated by her husband to marry another."[12]

Basil's rule concerns only the case of the husband who has dismissed his wife and the wife who has been dismissed. But what of the case where one spouse abandons the other? What may the abandoned spouse do? Basil says nothing about it here, but he does elsewhere in reply to questions put to him by one of his brother bishops, Amphilocius. First, he points out, the Lord's word applies equally to husbands and wives: they are both forbidden to abandon marriage except for adultery. But what of the case in which one abandons the other? What may the other do then? "The woman who leaves her husband is an adulteress if she goes to another husband. But the husband who is abandoned is worthy of pardon, and a woman who lives with him is not condemned. But if a husband who has dismissed his wife goes to another, he is an adulterer because he makes her commit adultery. And the woman who lives with him is an adulterer, because she has drawn to herself another's husband."[13]

While it recognized a gospel demand coming from the Lord, Basil's church showed compassion for innocent spouses, those who had been abandoned. That compassion resulted in a great reluctance to charge them with adultery if they remarried. That charge was reserved for a spouse who dismissed his or her partner and remarried, for a man who married a woman who had been dismissed by her husband for whatever reason, for a woman who married a man who had dismissed his wife unjustly, and also for a woman who dismissed her husband even justly and then remarried. Basil later reports the compassionate treatment of a husband who had abandoned his wife and remarried.

> The man who abandons the wife to whom he is legitimately married and marries another is, according to the Lord's judgment, subject to the condemnation of adultery. But it is established in the canons of our Fathers that such men should weep for a year, should be for two years among those who hear, for three years among those who prostrate themselves, and in the seventh year should be among the faithful, and thus by oblation render themselves worthy if they have done penance with tears.[14]

Here he sets out the conditions in his church for the return to full communion among the faithful of the man who has abandoned his wife. The second marriage seems to be accepted and the sending away of the second wife or the taking back of the first are not listed among the conditions for full communion.

John Chrysostom is regarded as the most influential teacher in the Eastern Church. His teaching about divorce and remarriage is as confused as is that of all his contemporaries. On the one hand, he warns wives that they must not leave their husbands, even if their marriage is intolerable. On the other hand, allowing that Paul has given wives a permission to leave, he allows that they may leave and are not obligated to return to their husbands, but that they must not remarry.[15] In his homily on First Corinthians 7 he sets forth the classic Judaeo-Christian ethic of the time: in the case of adultery spouses *must* separate. But he goes further, arguing that the adultery of the wife dissolves a marriage, leaving the husband no longer a husband.[16] In the Greek, for dissolve he uses the legal divorce word *dialuein*, which raises some very interesting questions. Does Chrysostom believe that the adultery of the wife, which is what he speaks of in his homily, or the adultery of the husband, which he does not speak of, dissolve their marriage in the very same way as a legal divorce? Can both then remarry, or at least the one not guilty of *porneia*? He does not say, and so we can only guess. What we can say with certainty is that the opinions of Basil and Chrysostom shaped the present practice of the Eastern Churches, which is that an *innocent* spouse in any divorce proceeding may be remarried in a church ceremony and incur no ecclesiastical penalty.

The doctrine and discipline in the Western or Roman Church is quite different. There, as we have seen, a marriage which is a Christian sacrament and consummated cannot be dissolved by any human authority. Consequently, any attempt at divorce is null and, therefore, any attempt at remarriage after divorce is null. We must now examine the source of that doctrine and discipline in two great Western Fathers.

In his commentary on Matthew's gospel, Jerome deals with the exceptive clause, *epi tes porneia*, except in the case of *porneia*. He explains that a wife's fornication (his translation of *porneia*) has put an end to the marital affection that exists in a marriage, and has rent the one-body union in two. The adulterous wife has separated herself from her husband, and he must separate from her lest he be condemned also. He quotes Proverbs 18:22: " 'Whoever keeps an adulterous wife is stupid and impious.' Wherever, therefore, there is fornication, and suspicion of fornication, a wife may be freely dismissed."[17] But what then? May the husband who has dismissed his wife because of adultery remarry? Jerome replies no, for the following reason. "It could happen that a man may falsely accuse an innocent wife, and because he wants a second marriage impute crime to the first. Therefore he is commanded to dismiss his first wife in such wise that he may take a second one while she lives." [18]

Jerome's meaning here is both clear and unclear. It is clear to the extent that he judges that a husband who has legitimately dismissed his wife may not remarry. But it is quite unclear why he may not remarry. Is he forbidden to remarry only to protect a possibly falsely accused wife? If it were demonstrated that the wife were guilty of adultery, could he then remarry? He does not answer here, but in an earlier letter to his friend Amandus he does clearly. Amandus had posed several questions to Jerome, among them one that asked if a woman who had left her husband on the grounds of adultery and sodomy and had been forced into a second marriage could participate in the life of the Church. Jerome's answer is short and unmistakably clear: "If a woman gives herself to another man while her husband is alive, she is an adulteress." [19] He claims this response is derived from Paul's words in Romans 7:1 and 1 Corinthians 7:39. And so there passed into Western Christian history an interpretation of the New Testament message: yes, indeed, a spouse may be dismissed for *porneia*, but such dismissal does not dissolve the marriage and enable either spouse to remarry another. It is but a separation, a separation from bed and board as the medievals would later say, claiming Jerome to their side.

Much more powerfully influential than Jerome on the marriage-divorce doctrine and discipline of the Roman Church was Augustine. His teaching is found most directly and systematically in a book, *On Adulterous Marriages*, he wrote in 419 to refute Pelagian errors. A Bishop Pollentius had his own interpretation of the New Testament data on divorce and remarriage. A husband and wife who are not guilty of adultery have these options: they may remain married; they may separate on the initiative of one of them who finds the marriage insupportable or who wishes to live a celibate life; if they do separate and then find a celibate life impossible, they may not remarry any other, but must return to one another. A husband or a wife whose spouse had committed adultery may divorce the spouse and remarry. In his reply, Augustine deals with each of these points in turn.

There is no question at all in a nonadulterous marriage. Where no adultery is involved, neither spouse may leave the marriage and certainly may not marry another. Only one reason justifies a spouse either to depart from a marriage or to dismiss the other spouse: the other's adultery. In this case, that is, when a spouse has left the other because of his or her adultery, even the innocent spouse must remain unremarried, exactly as Paul said.[20] He returns to and underscores these judgments in chapter six. "We say that, when both spouses are Christian, it is not permitted to a woman who has left her husband because of fornication to marry another, and it is not permitted to a woman under any circumstances to leave her husband who has not committed fornication."[21] Augustine, as did Jerome, apparently understood that the dismissal of a spouse for adultery, warranted both by Matthew's exceptive clause and by the well-accepted ethic of the early Christian Church, did not effect a true dissolution of the marriage but only a separation. So the Western tradition has understood him to mean.

This was not, of course, the first time Augustine had confronted the questions. He had confronted them in his commentary on the Sermon on the Mount. There are some points of interest for us in that document. He accepts the exceptive clause as coming from the Lord and insists on what we have already heard him saying.

> It is not permitted to dismiss a wife except on the ground of fornication. He (the Lord) obliges that a man remain with his wife if there is no fornication. If there is fornication, he does not oblige a man to send her away, but permits it. It is not permitted to the wife to marry another while her husband lives; if she does so, she sins. If after the death of her husband she does not marry, she does not sin, for she is not commanded to remarry, but permitted.[22]

Nothing strange so far.

But there is something very strange when Augustine asks about the nature of the fornication (which is his translation of the New Testament *porneia*). By weaving together Matthew's text and Paul's text in First Corinthians permitting an unbelieving spouse to depart from the marriage, he reaches the astounding conclusion that the fornication the Lord intended in the exceptive clause was the wife's religious, read non-Christian, infidelity. "If it is permitted to dismiss a non-believing spouse, although it is better not to dismiss him or her, and nevertheless it is not permitted according to the Lord's command to dismiss a spouse except on the ground of fornication, fornication is that very non-belief (*infidelitas*).[23] Augustine, astoundingly, interprets *porneia* to mean paganism. Because the

Lord only permitted the dismissal of a pagan wife or husband, and did not command it, Paul can come along later and permit a Christian husband or wife to remain with a pagan spouse.

There remains always the question of remarriage after dismissal. We have already heard him say that a wife must remain unmarried as long as her husband lives, and a husband must remain unmarried as long as his wife lives. But there is a case about which he professes to be doubtful. "If a wife is dismissed by her husband, with whom she wishes to remain, whoever marries her commits adultery, but whether she is guilty of the same crime is uncertain."[24] He does admit that it is hard to see how one spouse can be guilty of adultery and the other not, but the point of great interest here is that Augustine, not much given to hedged statements, does profess uncertainty. If he really believed unequivocally that dismissal of a spouse in every circumstance merely achieved a separation of the spouses, and not a dissolution of the marriage, would he have had such uncertainty?

In the earlier *The Good of Marriage*, directed against the Manichees, Augustine did not have that uncertainty. He asks whether, since the Scriptures permit a husband to dismiss his wife for adultery, the husband may remarry. He replies, first, that the Scriptures themselves make a "difficult knot" out of the question. Then, secondly, he gives a quite unequivocal answer. "I do not see how a man can have the freedom to marry another after dismissing an adulterous wife, since a woman does have the freedom to marry another after dismissing an adulterous husband." So strong is the bond between a married couple that "though it is entered into for the purpose of procreation, it is not loosed for the purpose of procreatin."[25] He justifies this teaching by drawing the whole question of marriage and divorce into his theology of the *sacramentum*. "I do not think it (the marriage bond) could have such strength unless it were some kind of *sacramentum* of something greater than would arise from our weak mortality, something that remains unshaken even in the face of men who desert this bond and attempt to dissolve it. The marriage bond is not dissolved by divorce so that, even though separated, the spouses remain married to one another, and both husband and wife commit adultery with those to whom they are married after divorce." At the end of it all, he makes a crucial explanatory statement: "but only in the City of God (Augustine's well-known figure for the Church), on his holy mountain, is such the case with a wife."[26]

Several things are now clear about Augustine's teaching. First, the marriage bond is such that even divorce does not dissolve it, not even divorce from a spouse guilty of fornication/adultery. Divorce, dismissal, abandonment achieves only a separation of the spouses, leaving them still married. Secondly, the resistance of the marriage bond to any effort to dissolve it is due to the fact that it is a *sacramentum* of something else. Thirdly, this *sacramentum* is found only within the City of God, the Christian Church. Only Christian marriages, therefore, are indissoluble. All that is clear.

One question remains. Of what is the marriage bond a *sacramentum* or symbol? Augustine is quite clear about the answer. "Just as the *sacramentum* of plural marriages in times gone by signified the future multitude of peoples on earth subject to God, so in our day the *sacramentum* of the monogamous marriage signifies the future unity of all of us subject to God in one heavenly city."[27] Marriage in the City of God, that is, marriage between Christians, is a sacrament or symbol for Augustine. But we need to be careful here. It is a sacrament, not of the present union of God and his people or of Christ and his Church, as we have frequently described it throughout this work, but of future unity between God and his people in the heavenly city. Later, in his *On Marriage and Concupiscence*, he will draw formally on the language of the letter to the Ephesians to speak of Christian marriage as a *sacramentum* of the unity between Christ and the Church.[28] Jerome's and Augustine's doctrine and the discipline flowing from it were bequeathed to the Western Church and, because of the prestige of these two thinkers, controlled not only its theology and its discipline, but also the very way it approached the reading and the interpretation of the Scriptures it held sacred. Since, as we have seen, the Western Church in our day holds only those marriages which are Christian sacrament and consummated as indissoluble, Augustine's theology of the *sacramentum*, however inchoately worked out, became of enduring significance.

Before leaving Augustine, we should glance briefly at the man who influenced him greatly, Ambrose of Milan. We shall find something of interest and something to illuminate the source of Augustine's teaching on the specialness of the marriage of two Christians. In his *Commentary on the Gospel of Luke*, Ambrose introduces the idea that not every marriage has been joined by God, and therefore not every marriage is under the injunction, "What God has joined together let not man put asunder." "There are those who think that every marriage is of God, especially because it is written, 'What God has joined together let not man put asunder.' If every marriage is of God, it is not permitted to dissolve any marriage. Why, then, has the Apostle said, 'If the unbelieving spouse departs, let him depart?' Admirably, he wished no motive for divorce to remain for Christians and showed that not every marriage is of God. For it is not by the judgment of God that Christian women marry pagans, since the law forbids this."[29]

Ambrose rejects a time-worn assumption and introduces a genuinely new twist to reflection on marriage and divorce—that every marriage is of God and, therefore, cannot be dissolved. The *novum* he introduces is that not every marriage is of God and, therefore, not every marriage is subject to the injunction to be not sundered. The conclusion he draws, calling Paul to his side, is that those marriages not of God can be dissolved by human authority. What marriages are not of God? Expressly, the marriage of a Christian woman and a pagan; implicitly, the marriage between two pagans. What marriages are of God and therefore indissoluble? The marriages of two Christians, or as Augustine would say later, marriages in the City of God.

To Roman Christians Ambrose gives clear instructions. "Do not dismiss your wife, lest you deny that God is the author of your marriage." "You dismiss your wife, as if you had a right to do so without fault. You think that is allowed because human law does not forbid it, but divine law forbids it. He who bows to men shames God."[30] And why are Christian marriages indissoluble? Because they are *sacramentum* of Christ and the Church. "The Apostle rightly warns," he writes, "that this is a great *sacramentum* of Christ and the Church. You will find a marriage, therefore, that no one can doubt is joined by God, since Jesus said, 'No one comes to me unless my Father who sent me draws him.' He (God) alone could join this marriage. Therefore Solomon said, in figure (*mystice*), 'a wife is prepared for a husband by God.' Christ is the husband, the Church the wife."[31] The marriage of two Christians is the great sacrament of the union between this husband and this wife. With such a mentor it is little wonder that Augustine speaks as he does.

Earlier in this book we met that great collector of opinions,

Gratian, and his distinction between initiated marriage and completed marriage. That distinction became the basis of his teaching on
the indissolubility and dissolubility of marriage. An initiated marriage, not yet completed by sexual intercourse, can be dissolved, and
the former spouses are quite free to remarry others. A marriage
completed by sexual intercourse is quite indissoluble, so that if the
spouses divorce, even if for the legitimate cause of adultery, the bond
of their marriage remains and neither is free to remarry. His judgment
on the question of indissolubility is beyond doubt. "Everything which
has been adduced concerning the non-dissolution of marriage is
understood of a completed marriage, one initiated by espousal and
consummated by the duty of sexual intercourse. What has been said
about a dissoluble marriage, on the other hand, is understood of an
initiated marriage, one which has not yet been consummated by the
fulfillment of that duty."[32] With this judgment, Gratian helped establish in the Roman Church the tradition that a marriage not yet
consummated by sexual intercourse may be dissolved.

Some 20 years after the compilation of Gratian's *Decree* at
Bologna, a theologian at Paris made yet another compilation, this
time of theological opinions. His name was Peter Lombard. His
compilation came to be known as the *Sententiae*, that is, opinions, of
Fathers, councils, popes, and theologians who preceded him. Despite
the fact that it is largely unoriginal, the *Sententiae* became an enor-
mously important work in medieval theology, one that subsequent
theologians had to cite obligatorily. The sole thing that concerns us
here, though, is what Lombard contributed to the Catholic tradition
of marriage and divorce. That contribution lies in his expansion of
Augustine's notion of the *sacramentum.*

Lombard accepts Augustine's three goods of marriage: faith,
offspring, sacrament. It is what he says of sacrament that is of interest
to us here, for he extends the meaning of it beyond what Augustine
intended. "Note," he teaches, "that the third good of marriage is
called *sacramentum*, not in the sense that it is the marriage itself, but
because the marriage is a sign of that very sacred reality which is the
spiritual and inseparable union of Christ and the church."[33] For
Augustine, *sacramentum* was the commitment of the spouses to one
another never to separate. For Lombard, it is a quality of the marriage, its quality as an image of the union of Christ and the Church.

A marriage, Lombard goes on to argue, can exist without the

fidelity of the spouses. It can exist without offspring. But it cannot exist without the *sacramentum*. "So inseparably founded in the marriage of legitimate persons is the *sacramentum* that it appears that without it there is no marriage, because there remains between them as long as they live the marriage bond. Even though there be divorce because of adultery, the firmness of the marriage bond is not dissolved."[34] Since it is the *sacramentum*, reflecting the union between Christ and the Church, that makes a marriage indissoluble, it is a small step to the conclusion that where there is no *sacramentum* a true marriage can be dissolved. With Lombard all the elements for the Roman Catholic approach to the question of dissolubility-indissolubility are now in place. From Gratian, only a marriage that is consummated is indissoluble. From Lombard, only a marriage that is sacramental, that reflects the union between Christ and the Church, is indissoluble. From these two positions will grow the modern Roman Catholic teaching: only the consummated, sacramental marriage is beyond every power to dissolve. But before considering that teaching as it appears in the *Code of Canon Law*, we must consider one more relevant medieval development in the area of marriage dissolubility.

We have just seen that Gratian judged the nonconsummated marriage to be dissoluble. That was not the only kind of marriage he thought was open to dissolution. He outlines this case. "A pagan man, who is married, is converted to the faith, and his wife out of hatred for the Christian faith leaves him. He takes a Christian woman for his wife, and when she dies he becomes a cleric." He then poses several questions, only two of which touch us here. "We ask, in the first place, whether there can be a marriage among pagans; and, secondly, whether he is permitted to take a second wife while his first wife lives?"[35] His answer to the first question is an important one. Yes, there is marriage among pagans. His answer to the second question employs a now-common distinction.

> It is one thing to dismiss a wife who wishes to remain in the marriage, and quite another not to follow a wife who departs from the marriage. It is permitted to dismiss a wife who wishes to remain in the marriage, but it is not permitted to marry another while she lives. A wife who departs need not be followed, and it is permitted to marry another while she lives. But this is to be understood only of those who married while they were pagans. But if both are converted to the faith, or if they

were married while they were Christians and after a time one abandons the faith and, out of hatred for the faith, the marriage, the abandoned spouse is not to live with the other. While she lives he cannot marry another, because the marriage between them was ratified, and such a marriage can in no way be dissolved.[36]

In the first part of his answer we can detect the elements of what Paul says in 1 Corinthians 7, and which came to be known in the developing Catholic tradition as the Pauline Privilege. In the second part, we can detect an agreement with Lombard's position. A couple married when both are Christians, and who have consummated their marriage as Christians, live in a ratified marriage, one that is sacramental. No matter what happens later, such a marriage is indissoluble. Several points of importance to our discussion here may be underscored. First, there is valid marriage among pagans, but it is not indissoluble marriage since it is not sacramental. Second, a valid pagan marriage may be dissolved when one of the spouses becomes a Christian, but only if the other spouse remains a pagan and departs from the marriage. Third, if the pagan spouse refuses to live with the now Christian partner and departs, the Christian is free to remarry according to church law. After Gratian, several popes will extend the scope of this Pauline Privilege, and a brief consideration of their rulings will bring us up to the present practice.

In the sixteenth century, circumstances in missionary Africa and the Indies forced upon Rome decisions extending the Pauline Privilege. The first of these decisions was made by Paul III in his apostolic constitution, *Altitudo*, issued in 1537. The decision looked to the case of pagan husbands in the Indies who were in polygamous marriages and who sought baptism. It prescribed that if the husband seeking to become a Christian could remember which of his wives he had married first, he was to keep her and dismiss all the others. But if he could not remember which wife he had married first, he could keep whichever wife he chose and dismiss all the others. In this latter case, the pope would dissolve the marriage between him and his "forgotten" first wife, so that both could then remarry without penalty.[37] Though this was treated at the time as an extension of the Pauline Privilege, we can note that it was much more than a simple extension. For the one characteristic which had consistently characterized the Pauline Privilege, from Paul's first articulation of it right up to the time of Paul III, that remarriage is permissible only in the case in which the pagan spouse departs, and not at all in the case in which she is dismissed, is now ignored. A husband is granted the privilege of retaining whichever wife he wishes and of dismissing all others.

In 1561, Pius V made yet another ruling in this case in his apostolic constitution, *Romani Pontificis*. He ruled that a converted polygamous husband could retain as his wife that one of his wives who was willing to receive baptism along with him. He ruled thus, moreover, as he explicitly states, *motu proprio*, on his own will and initiative, not on the basis of any biblical or theological or canonical tradition.

> Since several wives are permitted to the natives of the Indies when they are pagans, whom they repudiate even for the slightest of causes, it has come about that those husbands who receive baptism are permitted to remain with that wife who is baptized along with her husband. Since this woman often turns out not to be the first wife he married, both the ministers of the sacrament and bishops are tormented with scruples that this is not a true marriage. . . . Therefore, on our own initiative and from certain knowledge and the fullness of apostolic power, we declare . . . that those native Indians who have been baptized or who will be baptized may remain, as with their legitimate wife, with that woman who has been or who will be baptized with them, after dismissing all others. And with our apostolic authority we declare that such marriages between them are legitimate.[38]

Pius' ruling, claiming as it did that he had the power to specify which would be the legitimate wife of a converted polygamous husband and to dissolve all other marriages, including that of an unconverted first wife, was an enormous departure from established church law and practice. So enormous was it that canonists of the time urged that it be applied only in the case in which the genuinely first (and therefore presumedly legitimate) wife could not be found or identified. Such a procedure, they argued, would at least ensure that *known* consummated marriages would not be dissolved.

A final ruling touching our question was delivered in 1585 by Gregory XIII in his apostolic constitution, *Populis ac Nationibus*. Gregory's ruling looked to another problem, namely, the problem created when a husband or a wife is carried off into slavery and thereby separated from his or her spouse. What should happen if the now-separated spouse sought baptism and wished to marry again? The established procedure of the Pauline Privilege was to inquire from the pagan spouse whether he or she would live at peace with the newly converted Christian. In the case of the separation caused by enslavement, such an inquiry was not possible. Gregory granted a dispensation from the inquiry in such cases and exercised his claimed power to dissolve the previous pagan marriage. "We grant to local Ordinaries and Pastors . . . the power to dispense (from the inquiries) Christians of both sexes in the said territories, who have contracted marriage before being baptized and who have later converted to the faith. So that they may, even while their pagan spouse still lives, and even without his or her consent or waiting for his or her reply, legally contract marriage with any baptized person of any rite, solemnize such a marriage in the church, and legally remain in it after consummation as long as they live."[39]

All these rulings were considered at the time of their publication as extensions of the Pauline Privilege. But they go so far beyond the Pauline terms of that privilege that whether they are extensions of it or whether they are quite new privileges introduced by the papal power to bind and loose was and still is hotly disputed. Those who consider them an exercise of the power to bind and loose, and not an extension of the biblically warranted Pauline Privilege, name them the "Petrine Privilege."[40] Whatever one chooses to call them, however, such rulings and practices clarify one thing. They make clear that the Catholic claim that marriage is indissoluble is not to be understood as broadly as it appears on the surface. Rather it is to be interpreted as narrowly as it has been in both the theory and the practice of the Catholic Church. Only those marriages which are both sacramental and consummated are indissoluble.

Divorce and Remarriage in the Catholic Church: A Summation

Recently, I encountered this case. Two people who had been married twenty-eight years decided to separate. On talking to the husband, who is quite a religious man, I discovered that one of the great pains he was suffering was that he felt he could no longer participate in the sacramental life of the Church. The Catholic Church, he believed, does not allow married people to separate. I was able to tell him that he was quite wrong. Being separated or even being divorced does not cut off a Catholic from participation in the full life of the Church. Indeed, recognizing the pain and distress that separation or divorce often produces, the Church urges those who are in either situation to participate as fully as possible in sacramental life as a means of personal support. However much the failure of a marriage may be interpreted as a failure to live up to the gospel, and whether it is or is not such a failure is to be decided only in each individual circumstance, there is no canonical penalty for getting either a civil separation or a civil divorce. Civilly divorced Catholics incur canonical penalties only when they remarry while their previous spouse is still alive.

Notice, in the previous sentence, that I was careful to specify *civil divorce*. For, though the Catholic Church's reading of the gospel leads it to look upon all valid marriages as indissoluble, it does dissolve valid marriages. That is, it does grant divorces, under certain conditions, as we have seen. The most ancient of those "divorce" processes is the one known as the Pauline Privilege. Immediately after the apostle Paul reports in his letter to the Corinthians the Lord's command against divorce and remarriage, he allows an exception to that command in a case which is in question at Corinth. The Catholic Church has extended that exception into a process which it has called the Pauline Privilege, and which it has used extensively throughout its history in this circumstance. Two unbaptized persons are married; one of them now wishes to be baptized into the Catholic Church and the other refuses to live with him or her in peace; if the unbaptized spouse departs from the marriage, the church considers it dissolved and will issue a declaration to that effect. The final outcome is that both parties are now free to remarry. As we have seen, the Pauline Privilege has either been extended into the Petrine Privilege or has been added to by the Petrine Privilege on the basis of the assumed authority of the pope to bind and loose, even to loose valid marriages.

There is yet another way to dissolve a valid marriage in the Catholic Church. The ancient Roman answer to the question of when did a marriage actually take place was that it took place when the marrying couple freely consented to be married. The northern European answer was that it took place when the couple engaged in their first sexual intercourse after the giving of that consent. The medieval Church combined these two opinions and taught that a marriage was *initiated* by consent and *consummated* by sexual intercourse. If, after the giving of consent, which initiates a valid marriage, there has been no sexual intercourse, then the marriage may be dissolved or a Church "divorce" may be granted. Both parties are now free to remarry without any Church penalty.

Besides these ways to dissolve a marriage in the Catholic Church, there is that other famous (or perhaps infamous) procedure known as annulment. Now annulment is quite a different procedure from the dissolution procedures, for while these dissolve the bond of a marriage that is believed to be valid, annulment is a judgment that there never was at any time a valid marriage bond between these two people. It is common knowledge that today Church annulments are granted more frequently than ever before. In 1969, about 700 annulments were granted in the United States; in 1979, that number had risen fortyfold to about 28,000. In 1984, thanks to new procedural norms and to the broadening of grounds for annulment, some church lawyers feel that virtually every failed marriage that comes before a Church tribunal can be annulled. That feeling has become so pervasive that it has also become a source of controversy within the Church, some arguing that granting an annulment has become too easy, others arguing that it should be liberalized even further to respond to the needs of hurting people, and still others arguing that the tribunals are doing more harm than good.

Grounds for annulment are multiple: lack of the proper form decreed by *Tametsi*, Catholics marrying without the presence of a designated priest and two witnesses; lack of intention to have children; somehow defective consent, as a result, for instance, of grave fear or force; prior intention to be unfaithful; prior mental illness or alcoholism or psychosexual problems; general immaturity at the time of the marriage. It has been calculated that the lack of due discretion, also called psychic incapacity, psychic irregularity, moral impotency, is involved in about ninety percent of the annulment cases that come before tribunals, leading some canon lawyers to suggest that virtually every failed marriage can be annulled on that basis.

In chapter three I discussed at length the essential need for Christian faith to transform human marriage into Christian sacrament. Here, then, I need recall only briefly that where that faith is lacking from the beginning there is valid human marriage, but not valid Christian sacrament. And where there is not sacramental marriage, there is not indissoluble marriage. We know that the official documents of the Roman Catholic Church, including the revised *Code of Canon Law*, state a quite different position, and that the present practice of the Catholic Church based on those documents is also in conflict with what I have argued. But we know also the conflict between traditional Roman Catholic theology and law on this point. The church would never admit to the sacrament of baptism an adult who claimed that he had no Christian faith. Why then, and how, would it admit such an adult to the sacrament of marriage? If it delays baptism so that Christian faith can be ensured, and it does, why can it not delay sacramental marriage for the same reason and permit in the meantime a valid civil marriage with all its marital rights and responsibilities? This is the approach suggested, and practiced, by the French bishops mentioned at the beginning of this book. I admit freely that there are complexities in the question that do not admit of easy answers. That is why, I believe, the law of the Church which seeks legal precision has not yet been brought into line with its theology. But law has a long history of simplifying complexities, and I am confident that it will do so again in this case.[41]

That vast array of Church and canonical possibility notwithstanding, it is no secret that many Roman Catholic marriages, somewhere in the region of thirty percent of them, end in civil divorce. Nor is it any secret that many of those civilly divorced Catholics enter into second marriages which, since they are looked upon by the Church as irregular marriages, bring with them canonical penalties such as a bar from participating in the sacramental life of the Church. Many Roman Catholic theologians, canon lawyers, ministers, and lay people are asking a new question today. Is there anything that the Church can do to minister today to those in such irregular marriages, beyond pointing out the demands of a gospel life or repeating that the law is the law? In May 1977, the Catholic bishops of the United States asked the Vatican and were granted permission to drop the automatic excommunication for civilly divorced Catholics who remarry while their previous spouse is still alive. That was an apparently small, but in symbolic reality a momentous, gesture, for it removed one source of pain for many Catholics. Can any more be done?

The breakdown of a marriage is always a human tragedy, causing hurt to husband, wife, children, family, and friends. When a marriage fails, within the very context in which most people seek love and trust and security, they find hatred, distrust, and much insecurity.

It is for this reason, for the hurts that it causes, that divorce is an evil in the human community, and is forbidden by God. We miss this point, and put the cart before the horse when we think that divorce is evil just because it is forbidden. Kelly points out, summoning Aquinas to his side, that "God is not offended by us except insofar as we harm ourselves and other people. Marriage breakdown and divorce is evil because of the human hurt and suffering caused by it. It offends God because people precious to him are being harmed and are hurting each other."[42] Canon lawyers point out frequently that each time the Roman Catholic Church dissolves a marriage it is for a good judged to be greater than the good of indissolubility, namely, the salvation of souls. In an address to the Sacred Roman Rota, Pius XII validated such a position. "In every case," he argued, "the supreme norm according to which the Roman Pontiff makes use of his vicarious power to dissolve a marriage is . . . the salvation of souls, in the attainment of which both the common good of the religious society, and of human society in general, and the good of individuals find due and proportionate consideration."[43] The present pope, John Paul II, when still Archbishop Wojtyla, argued that to defend and to preserve the deposit of faith "entails its growing understanding, in tune with the demands of every age and responding to them according to the progress of theology and human science."[44] Some contemporary Roman Catholic theologians are asking whether such arguments might extend to the question of divorce and remarriage. They are also suggesting some possibilities.

First, there is the ancient practice of the Eastern Church, going back, as we saw, to Basil and John Chrysostom. While holding firmly to the belief that the gospel presents a demand for indissoluble marriage, it acknowledges also that real men and women sometimes do not measure up to the gospel. It acknowledges that human marriages, and even specifically Christian marriages, do end and that when they end it makes no sense to insist that they are still binding ontologically. It seeks then to deal in a pastorally compassionate way with the former married spouses, even to the extent of allowing the remarriage of an *innocent spouse*. The second marriage is not put on a par, however, with the first one, and its liturgical celebration makes this quite clear. It is not the joyful and glorious liturgy of the first marriage, but one dominated by notes of sorrow for a previous failure and of repentance for the same, reflecting the ever-present paradox of grace and sin, Christian ideal and human frailty, and the Church's role as minister to both.

The Roman Catholic Church which itself has canonical processes to dissolve a valid marriage, has never condemned this Eastern practice. Even the Council of Trent, which appeared to take a hardline approach to the question of indissolubility, worded its canon on indissolubility very carefully so as not to offend the Easterns. It refused deliberately to state that the Eastern practice did not have equal claim to the gospel tradition and to the name Christian.[45] Some Roman Catholic theologians are asking whether the Eastern practice might provide a basis for a change in pastoral attitude toward the divorced and remarried in the Roman Catholic Church. Indeed, at the Synod of Bishops held in Rome in 1980, one of the forty-three propositions presented to the pope was one which asked explicitly that the practice of the Eastern Church in this matter be carefully studied for the illumination it might shed on Roman practice. Fidelity to Jesus' prohibition of remarriage does not mean that the Church cannot make pastoral provision for the spiritual welfare of those who have entered second marriages, many of which have become so stable that they cannot be broken without grave economic, emotional, and spiritual harm to the parties involved.

Secondly, there is another, ancient Catholic factor which must come into the reckoning in the question of civil divorce and remarriage. When a marriage case is settled in a marriage tribunal, it is said to be settled *in foro externo*, in the external forum. But there is an ancient Catholic tradition which insists that, under certain conditions, questions of sin and non-sin are settled ultimately *in foro interno*, in the internal forum, the forum of good conscience and good faith. In the case of civil divorce and remarriage such an approach means this: that when divorced Catholics, whose first spouse is still alive and whose first marriage has not been annulled, enter a second marriage with an honest and conscientious decision, the Church can and does accept their decision of conscience, cannot and does not consider them sinners, and cannot and does not bar them from full participation in the sacramental life of the Church. In the confused situation of the post-Vatican II Church, unfortunately, couples wishing to explore this internal forum solution will encounter both priests who will counsel them to follow their own conscience and priests who will counsel that such a solution cannot be applied in their case. In both cases, however, the Church teaches, the bottom line is not the priest's counsel but the couple's honest decision of conscience to share or not to share in the full sacramental life of the Church.

Certain conditions, of course, must be fulfilled for either of these two approaches to come into play. The following are among the most crucial and most frequently listed: 1) none of the present canonical solutions can be applied in the case in question; 2) the first marriage must be irretrievably ended and reconciliation impossible (an uncontested divorce, refusal of one party to be reconciled, new obligations toward children in the second marriage may be taken as signs that a first marriage is dead); 3) obligations deriving from a first marriage must be accepted and reasonably discharged (reasonable child support, alimony, property settlement, acceptance of personal responsibility for the failure of the first marriage and sorrow for any sin in that failure are among such obligations); 4) obligations deriving from the second marriage must be responsibly accepted and discharged, and the couple must show that in the second marriage they intend to live a stable marriage in a church community (the birth of children, the stability of the second marriage over a period of years, the desire to participate in the full life of the Church are all good indications of responsible sincerity); 5) the desire for the sacraments must be motivated by genuine Christian faith, which we do well to presume is present in those who are sincerely pained by being barred from normal participation in the sacraments.

For the moment, these two approaches to dealing with the question of divorce and remarriage in the Roman Catholic Church are very much in the early stages of theoretical speculation. But that is one of the functions of theological thinkers in the church, to uncover all the possible options in the ancient Catholic tradition. Theologians do not make decisions for the Church, but merely uncover for it the theological and pastoral options which are open to it in its own tradition, inviting it to ponder them and discern its future directions. It is precisely that process of uncovering and inviting to discern that Roman Catholic theologians are engaged in presently.

Summary

This chapter has been about the theory and the practice of marriage, divorce, and remarriage in the Roman Catholic Church. First, it sought to explain that the popular wisdom about divorce and remarriage in that tradition is a little simplistic and, to that extent, more than a little wide of the mark. The position of the Roman Church, as it may be culled from the historical practice of that Church, is abundantly clear. Only that marriage which is consummated as Christian sacrament is indissoluble; all other kinds not only are dissoluble but also have been dissolved by the Roman Catholic Church at one time or another in its history. Secondly, the chapter looked at the words about divorce and remarriage in the New Testament. It found a universal memory of Jesus' teaching about divorce and remarriage, a teaching articulated in the parable saying: "Every one who divorces his wife and marries another commits adultery." It found also interpretations of Jesus' parable by Mark, Matthew, and Paul and exceptions allowed by Matthew for *porneia* and by Paul in the case that came to be known in history as the Pauline Privilege. It found also that, in its long history, the Catholic Church has dissolved unquestionably valid marriages on the basis of either the Pauline Privilege, or its companion Petrine Privilege, or the nonconsummation of the marriage.

Thirdly, the chapter alluded to that procedure known as annulment, in which the Roman Catholic Church declares that in a given marriage there never was a valid marriage bond. It listed reasons on the basis of which an annulment might be granted and commented on the incredibly increased use of this procedure in the dioceses of the United States. Finally, the chapter called attention to the large numbers of Roman Catholics who are in the painful position of being divorced, or divorced and remarried, and asked the pressing question of what the Church of Christ could do to minister pastorally to them in our day.

Questions for Reflection and Discussion

1. Given the history of its practice, is it accurate to say that the Roman Catholic Church never grants divorces? Is there any difference between a divorce and a dissolution of a marriage? If there is, what is it?

2. Can you explain clearly the difference between the dissolution of a

marriage and an annulment? Do you really see them as quite different?

3. If a marriage establishes a blood relationship, as it does in the time of Jesus, how could it be dissolved? Do we look upon marriage in our time as establishing a blood relationship? If we do not, does the saying of Jesus about divorce and remarriage apply to us? How?

4. How did you react when you read that the saying of Jesus about divorce and remarriage "has to be a parable?" If it is a parable, what difference would it make? If it is not a parable, which of the New Testament versions of it should the Church follow?

5. What are your reactions to the practice of the Eastern Church with respect to the innocent party in a divorce proceeding? Does it seem to you that the practice is pastorally applicable in the Roman Catholic Church? What do you believe should be the attitude in the church to those who have been divorced and remarried while their original spouse is still alive?

Afterword

This book is about not every marriage celebrated in the human community, but only marriage celebrated and consummated as Christian sacrament and named, therefore, *Christian* marriage. Christian marriage is a marriage in which two baptized believers consent to be united not only to become one body-person, but also to become a prophetic symbol of the union between Christ and his Church. It is a marriage in which their sacred scriptures urges Christians to love one another steadfastly in mutual loyalty, service and obedience. It is a marriage which Ambrose declared to be of God, Augustine declared to be in the City of God, and medieval theologians, finally, judged to be a sacrament, that is, both a sign and a cause of grace. It is a marriage in which believing Christian spouses celebrate and make real not only their love for one another, but also their love for Jesus the Christ and the God whom he reveals as Grace. It is a marriage in which they live in the presence not only of one another, but also of grace, and thereby come to holiness and salvation.

Christian marriage, the marriage consummated as explicit Christian sacrament, is not the only kind of valid marriage in the human community. But it is the only valid marriage that the Roman Catholic Church judges to be indissoluble. Valid marriages which are nonsacramental it dissolves; valid marriages which are nonconsummated it dissolves. Valid marriages between those who have been baptized and which it judges to have been invalid from the beginning are annulled for a variety of reasons, most of which have to do with the contractual nature of marriage. This book shows that there is at least one reason that invalidates the Christian, sacramental nature of the marriage, the lack of Christian faith. Sadly, lack of faith is a fact today not only among those who have not been baptized, but also among many who have been baptized but who have never come to Christian faith. This book argued that such baptized nonbelievers ought never to be equated with Christian believers in Roman Catholic law, theology, or practice.

The Roman Catholic sacramental tradition is consistently and abundantly clear; nonbelievers do not and cannot celebrate valid Christian sacrament. The Roman Catholic Church needs to take that tradition seriously today, so that it itself might be taken seriously as a depository of consistent truth. It needs to acknowledge that where all the elements for a valid marriage are present and all the elements for a valid sacrament are not present, then there is valid marriage and not mere concubinage, but not valid sacrament. It needs to admit, as did those bishops in France whose experiment served as the preface to this book, that this is true of all nonbelievers, baptized or not.

This book sought also to set in focus what is no secret to any contemporary Christian, namely, that some thirty per cent of marriages between baptized Roman Catholics, many of whom are baptized believers, end in civil divorce and that many of these divorced Catholics remarry while their previous spouse is still alive. It is such remarriage that Matthew suggests is forbidden in Jesus' parable saying: "Every one who divorces his wife . . . and marries another commits adultery" (19:9). While, on the one hand, acknowledging the saying of Jesus and its legitimacy, the Eastern Churches, on the other hand, have long permitted the remarriage of divorced spouses under certain controlled conditions. The Western Churches have always condemned such remarriage, though they have never condemned the Eastern practice and they have never suggested that it did not merit the name *Christian*. Some Roman Catholic theologians today are asking whether that Eastern practice might offer a direction in which the Roman Catholic Church might find a compassionate pastoral approach toward its own divorced and remarried members.

Theologians, of course, do not make decisions for their Church. They have a quite different task, that "of interpreting the documents of the past and present magisterium, of putting them in the context of the whole of revealed truth, and of finding a better understanding of them by the use of hermeneutics."[1] That task, as I acknowledged at the outset, brings with it a somewhat critical and, therefore, risky function. It is precisely such a task of interpreting and better understanding the total, and not just a selected, Catholic tradition about divorce and remarriage that Roman Catholic theologians are engaged in presently. It should be clear from everything that has been said throughout this book that the total Catholic tradition is actually quite clear. On the one hand, there is the interpretation of Jesus' parable about divorce and remarriage that judges that marriage is indissoluble and that, therefore, remarriage after divorce and while one's previous spouse still lives is invalid. On the other hand, even in the Roman Catholic tradition, there is the dissolution of admittedly valid marriages or annulment of those which are judged to have been never valid.

That Church which is the body of Christ is required to reflect always on the words of its Lord. There is one I find apposite here: "The sabbath was made for man, not man for the sabbath" (Mark 2:27). Such a saying has implications, I believe, not only for questions about the sabbath, but also for questions about many things, including divorce and remarriage. I believe also that an approach such as that of the Eastern Church represents an effort to be responsive pastorally to the concerns embedded in such a saying. A cry of pain continues to be heard in the Churches. "He who is able to receive this, let him receive it" (Matthew 19:12).

Notes

Abbreviations

AAS: *Acta Apostolicae Sedis: Commentarium Officiale* (Roma: Typis Polyglottis Vaticanis)

CBQ: *The Catholic Biblical Quarterly* (The Catholic Biblical Association of America)

DS: *Enchiridion Symbolorum Definitionum et Declarationum de Rebus Fidei et Morum,*ed. H. Denzinger et A. Schoenmetzer (Editio 33 emendata et aucta; Freiburg: Herder, 1965)

DV: *The Documents of Vatican II,* ed. Walter M. Abbott (London: Chapman, 1966)

MD: *La Maison Dieu* (Paris: Cerf)

PG: *Patrologiae Cursus Completus: Series Graeca,* ed. J. P. Migne

PL: *Patrologiae Cursus Completus: Series Latina,* ed. J. P. Migne

ST: *Summa Theologiae Sancti Thomae de Aquino* (Roma: Editiones Paulinae, 1962)

TS: *Theological Studies* (Washington: Georgetown University)

WOR: *Worship* (Collegeville: Liturgical Press)

1. All abbreviations in the Notes are listed without any underlined emphasis.

2. All translations from languages other than English are the author's.

Introduction

1. English report in James A. Schmeiser, "Marriage: New Alternatives," WOR 55 (1981), 23–34.

2. See "Propositions on the Doctrine of Christian Marriage," in *Origins,* September 28, 1978, 237.

3. *Declaration on Religious Freedom,* n.7, DV, 686.

4. International Theological Commission, *Theses on the Relationship Between the Ecclesiastical Magisterium and Theology* (Washington: United States Catholic Conference, 1977), 6.

Chapter One

1. For more detailed information see M. Eliade, *Patterns in Comparative Religion* (London: Sheed and Ward, 1979); E. O. James, *The Cult of the Mother-Goddess* (London: Thames and Hudson, 1959).

2. E. Schillebeeckx, *Marriage: Secular Reality and Saving Mystery,* Vol. 1 (London: Sheed and Ward, 1965), 39.

3. F. R. Barry, *A Philosophy from Prison* (London: SCM, 1926), 151. Cp. Schillebeeckx, *Marriage,* 43; Markus Barth, *Ephesians: Translation and Commentary on Chapters Four to Six. The Anchor Bible* (New York: Doubleday, 1974), 734–738; X. Leon-Dufour (ed.), *Vocabulaire de Theologie Biblique,* 2nd ed. rev. (Paris: Cerf, 1970), 146-152.

4. See Richard Batey, "The *mia sarx* Union of Christ and the Church," *New Testament Studies* 13 (1966–67), 272.

5. For a discussion of whether the term *myth* should be applied to any biblical passage, and for a suggestion of alternative language, see John McKenzie, "Myth and the Old Testament," CBQ 21 (1959), 265–282.

6. William L. Moran, "The Ancient Near Eastern Background of the Love of God in Deuteronomy," CBQ 25 (1963), 82.

7. Bruce J. Malina, *The New Testament World: Insights from Cultural Anthropology* (Atlanta: John Knox, 1981), 110.

8. It is of no interest to any thesis in this book whether the Apostle Paul was or was not the author of Ephesians, and so I do not deal with that disputed question, referring only to *the writer.* Those who require information on the question may consult any of the modern commentaries.

9. Markus Barth, *Ephesians,* 607.

10. *The Jerusalem Bible* (London: Darton, Longman and Todd, 1966).

11. *The Holy Bible: Revised Standard Version* (London: Nelson, 1959).

12. Barth, *Ephesians,* 609.

13. Heinrich Schlier, *Der Brief an die Epheser* (Dusseldorf: Patmos, 1962), 252.

14. J. Paul Sampley, *And the Two Shall Become One Flesh: A Study of Traditions in Ephesians 5:21-33* (Cambridge: University Press, 1971), 119-121.

15. Barth, *Ephesians,* 607.

16. Ibid., 618.

17. Cf. Sampley, *The Two Shall Become One Flesh,* 33.

18. Cf. ibid., 30. See 30-34; cp. Barth, *Ephesians,* 704-708.

19. Thedore Mackin, *What is Marriage?* (New York: Paulist, 1982), 56.

20. Cited in Paul F. Palmer, "Christian Marriage: Contract or Covenant? " TS 33 (1972): 647-648.

Chapter Two

1. *Epist. ad Diognetum,* 5, PG 2,1173.

2. *Stromatum* 3, 5, PG 8, 1143-1147.

3. Ibid. 3, 13, PG 8, 1191.

4. Ibid. 3, 12, PG 8, 1186.

5. *Adv. Haer.* 1, 28, 1, PG 7, 690.

6. *Stromatum* 3, 17, PG 8, 1206.

7. Ibid. 2, 23, PG 8, 1086. See also *Paed.* 2, 10, PG 8, 498: "For those who are joined in marriage, its scope and purpose is the reception of children."

8. Ibid. 2, 23, PG 8, 1090.

9. Ibid. 3, 12, PG 8, 1184.

10. Ibid. 2, 23, PG 8, 1090–1091.

11. Ibid. 4, 19, PG 8, 1333.

12. Cf. Ibid. 3, 2 PG 8, 1103–1111; *Adv. Haer.* 1, 25, PG 7, 680–686.

13. *Divinarum Institutionum* 6, 23, PL 6, 718.

14. *Apologia Prima pro Christianis* 1, 29, PG 6, 374.

15. *Stromatum* 3, 7, PG 8, 1162.

16. *In Gen. Hom.* 3, 6, PG 12, 180.

17. Ibid. 5, 4, PG 12, 192.

18. *Didascalia Apostolorum* 6, 28, in *The Ante-Nicene Fathers* (New York: Schribner's, 1913), Vol. VII, 463.

19. *Expositio Evang. sec. Lucam* 3, par. 43–46, PL 15, 1550–1552.

20. *Comment.in Epist. ad Galatas* 3, 5, PL 26, 415.

21. Cora E. Lutz, *Musonius Rufus: The Roman Socrates* (New Haven: Yale University Press, 1947). Cited from facsimile by Xerox University Microfilms, Ann Arbor, 1975, 87.

22. *Contra Celsum* 3, 66, PG 11, 1006.

23. *Ad Uxorem I,* 2–3, PL 1, 1277–79.

24. *Ad Uxorem II,* 9, PL 1, 1302–1303.

25. *De Pud.* 16, PL 2, 2, 1012.

26. *Constitution on the Church in the Modern World,* n. 48, DV 250–252.

27. See, for instance, Louis Bouyer, *The Seat of Wisdom: An Essay on the Place of the Virgin Mary in Christian Theology* (Chicago:

Regnery, 1965), 73, 75.

28. *De Haeresibus* 46, PL 42, 37.

29. *De Nuptiis et Concup.* 2, 32, 54, PL 44, 468–469. See also *De Bono Coniugali,* passim, PL 40, 374–396.

30. *De Gen. ad Litt.* 9, 7, 12, PL 34, 397; see also *De Bono Coniug.* 24, 32, PL 40, 394; *De Pecc. Originali* 34, 39, PL 44, 404; *De Nupt.et Concup.* 1, 17, 19, PL 44, 424; *Contra Julianum Pelagianum* 5, 12, 46, PL 44, 810. For an extended analysis and bibliography see A. Reuter, *Sancti Aurelii Augustini Doctrina de Bonis Matrimonii. Analecta Gregoriana,* Vol. 27 (Rome: Gregorian University Press, 1942).

31. *De Bono Coniug.* 9, 9, PL 40, 380; see Ibid., PL 40, 378.

32. Cap.3, PL 40, 375.

33. Cap. 9, PL 40, 380.

34. *De Sermone Domini in Monte* 1, 15, 42, PL 34, 1250.

35. Theodore Mackin, *What is Marriage?* (New York: Paulist, 1982), 141.

36. I call attention to two rather well-known cases. The first is in John T. Noonan's influential book, *Contraception: A History of its Treatment by the Catholic Theologians and Canonists* (Cambridge: Harvard University Press, 1965). There, ignoring the texts cited in footnotes 32, 33, 34, he claims that Augustine makes no mention of love between the spouses in his treatment of the goods of marriage (126–131). The second is Derrick S. Bailey's *Sexual Relations in Christian Thought* (New York: Harper, 1959), in which he claims that the seventeenth century Anglican divine, Jeremy Taylor, makes what is "probably the first express recognition in the theological literature of what may be termed the relational purpose of coitus" (208).

37. *Retractationes,* 1, 15, 2, PL 32, 608.

38. *Contra Julianum Pelag.* 3, 23, 53, PL 44, 729–30.

39. *De Bono Coniug.* 6, 6, PL 40, 377–378; ibid. 10, 11, PL 40, 381; *De Coniug. Adult.* 2, 12, PL 40, 479; *Contra Julian.Pelag.* 2, 7, 20, PL 44 687.

40. *De Bono Coniug.* 16, 18, PL 40, 386.

41. Ibid., 6, 5, PL 40, 377.

42. *Epistolarum Liber IX,* Epist. 64, PL 77, 1196.

43. Edward Schillebeeckx, *Ministry: Leadership in the Community of Jesus Christ* (New York: Crossroad, 1981), 88–89.

44. ST, III (Suppl.), 65, 1, corp.

45. Ibid., 1, 98, 2 ad 3.

46. Ibid., III (Suppl.), 41, 3 ad 6.

47. Ibid., corp.; cp. *Contra Gentiles,* 3, 126; IIa IIae, 153, 2.

48. Ibid., ad 1.

49. Ibid., III (Suppl.), 41, 4; Ibid., 49, 5.

50. IIa IIae, 142, 1.

51. E.C. Messenger, *Two in One Flesh. Part 2: The Mystery of Sex in Marriage* (London: Sands, 1948), 178–179.

52. *Sententiae,* 4, d.1, c.4.

53. Ibid., 4, d.2, c.1.

54. Ibid., 4, d.26, c.6.

55. *Commentarium in Libros Sententiarum,* 4, d.26, a.14, q.2 ad 1.

56. *Commentum in Quartum Librum Sententiarum,* d.26, q.2, a.3, repeated in *Suppl.,* 42, 3c.

57. *Contra Gentiles,* 4, 78.

58. DS 718.

59. DS 761.

60. DS 860.

61. DS 1310.

62. DS 1327.

63. Cf. DS 1601, 1606, 1801, 1802, 1807.

64. Anyone wishing the detail can consult Mackin, *What is Marriage?*, 145–175.

65. *Decretum,* Pars II, Causa XXVII, Quaestio II, Cap. 34, PL 187, 1406.

66. *Codex Iuris Canonici* (1917), Can. 1015,1; *Codex Iuris Canonici* (1983), Can. 1061,1.

67. *Epist.XXII,* PL 126, 145.

68. DS 1813–1816.

Chapter Three

1. *Catechism of the Council of Trent for Priests,* trans. J. Donovan (Rome: Propaganda Fide Press, 1839), 641.

2. Ibid., 643.

3. Ibid., 661.

4. Ibid., 653.

5. David E. Fellhauer, "The *Consortium Omnis Vitae* as a Juridical Element of Marriage," *Studia Canonica,* Vol. 13,1: 82. See 81–82.

6. Urban Navarrette, "Structura Juridica Matrimonii Secundum Concilium Vaticanum II," *Periodica* 56 (1967), 366.

7. Mackin, *What is Marriage?,* 214.

8. Gerald C. Treacy (ed.), *Five Great Encyclicals* (New York: Paulist, 1939), 83–84.

9. Dietrich von Hildebrand, *Marriage* (London: Longman's, Green and Co., 1942), v.

10. Ibid., vi.

11. Ibid., 4.

12. Ibid., 6.

13. Ibid., 25. Emphasis in original.

14. Heribert Doms, *The Meaning of Marriage,* trans. George Sayer (London: Sheed and Ward, 1939), 94–95.

15. AAS 36 (1944), 103.

16. Ibid., 43 (1951), 848–849.

17. See *Commentary on the Documents of Vatican II,* Vol. 5 (New York: Herder and Herder, 1969), 225.

18. *Acta et Documenta Concilio Vaticano II Apparando.* Series II (Praeparatoria), Vol.II, Pars III (Roma:Typis Polyglottis Vaticanis, 1968), 937.

19. Ibid., 910, par. 16, and 917, note 50.

20. Ibid., 909.

21. Those who wish to learn about that convoluted history may consult either Charles Moeller, "History of the Constitution," in *Commentary on the Documents of Vatican II,* Vol.5, 1–76; or Theodore Mackin, *What is Marriage?,* 248–278. Citations from the document are from DV, 249–255.

22. Cited in Haring, loc.cit., 234.

23. Cited in Paul F. Palmer, "Christian Marriage: Contract or Covenant?," TS 33 (1972), 647–648.

24. Vol. III, Part 4 (Edinburgh: Clark, 1961), 186.

Chapter Four

1. Juan Alfaro, "Faith," in *Sacramentum Mundi: An Encyclopedia of Theology* (New York: Herder, 1968), II:315.

2. DS 1532.

3. DS 1529.

4. "Huius iustificationis causae sunt:....instrumentalis item

sacramentum baptismi, quod est 'sacramentum fidei' *sine qua* nulli umquam contigit iustificatio." Emphasis added.

5. DS 1606.

6. DS 1310.

7. *Constitution on the Sacred Liturgy,* n.59, DV, 158.

8. ST III, 49, 3 ad 1.

9. *Pastoral Constitution on the Church in the Modern World,* n.48, DV, 250.

10. "Christian Marriage: Contract or Covenant," TS 33 (1972), 639.

11. *Church in the Modern World,* nn. 47–48, DV, 249–252.

12. *Dogmatic Constitution on the Church,* n.11, DV, 29.

13. Those who wish to survey the opinions may consult; *Foi et sacrement de mariage* (Paris: Chalet, 1974); Edward Kilmartin, "When is Marriage a Sacrament?," TS 34 (1973), 275–286; Jean-Marie Aubert, "Foi et Sacrement dans le mariage," MD (1970), 116–143; William Marrevee, "Is a Marriage 'in the Church' a Marriage 'in the Lord'?" *Eglise et Theologie* 8 (1977), 91–109; James A. Schmeiser, "Marriage: New Alternatives," WOR 55 (1981), 23–34; Francis Morrissey, "Revising Church Legislation on Marriage," *Origins* 9 (1979-80), 211–218. It is noteworthy that French theologians and canon lawyers, confronted by a great mass of *baptized nonbelievers* (See "Propositions on the Doctrine of Christian Marriage," in *Origins,* Sept. 28, 1978, 237), have made sustained efforts to elaborate theological and canonical theories to ground such a concerted practice. The English-speaking churches, undoubtedly faced with the same problem, would do well to confront the problem from within their own cultural situations.

14. DS 1801. Emphasis added.

15. A. Duval, "Contrat et sacrement de mariage au Concile de Trente," MD 127 (1976), 50.

16. DS 2991. Emphasis added.

17. DS 3145. Emphasis added.

18. Duval, "Contrat et Sacrement," 63.

19. Cf. ST III, 60, 3; III, 62, 1; III, 63, 3.

20. See above, note 13.

21. I use the words *sacrament* and *sacramental* here with their technical Roman Catholic meanings. I have no problem, however, with the extended meanings given to the words by J. de Baciochhi, who argues that even the marriages of pagans, nonbelievers and divorced and remarried are "sacramental." See his "Propositions au sujet du mariage des baptises non croyants," in *Foi et sacrement de mariage,* 110–116. See also the comments of the International Theological Commission in "Propositions on the Doctrine of Christian Marriage," in *Origins,* Sept. 28, 1978, 237–238.

22. The well-known judgment of the *Letter to Diognetus* that Christians "marry like everyone else" shows that Christians did not initially abandon their ancestral ways of marrying (PG 2, 1173). See also CIC (1917), Can. 1098, and CIC (1983), Can. 1116. The *Code*'s granting of a dispensation from the presence of a designated priest in the case in which a couple would have to wait a month for him to be present seriously weakens the claim that his presence is required for validity.

23. See *La Documentation Catholique,* Dec. 7, 1969, 1075–1077; also James E. Schmeiser, "Marriage: New Alternatives," WOR 55 (1981), 23–34.

24. AAS 59 (1967), 166.

25. *Constitution on the Church in the Modern World,* n.36, DV, 233.

26. Ibid., n.76, 288.

27. *Declaration on Religious Freedom,* n.10, DV, 689–690. Emphasis added.

28. Much like the meaning assigned to it, for instance, by Michael Novak in *Ascent of the Mountain, Flight of the Dove: An Invitation to Religious Studies* (New York: Harper & Row, 1978).

29. See John Giles Milhaven, "Conjugal Sexual Love and Contemporary Moral Theology," TS 35 (1974), 704–705.

30. "On Taking Sex Seriously," in *Moral Issues and Christian Response,* P. Jersild and D. Johnson, ed. (New York: Holt, Rinehart, Winston, 1971), 102–104.

31. John Giles Milhaven, "Conjugal Sexual Love," n.15, 700.

32. Ibid., 705.

33. The ideas articulated in this section on *eros* and *agape* were stimulated by Helmut Gollwitzer's beautiful little book, *Song of Love: A Biblical Understanding of Sex* (Philadelphia: Fortress, 1979).

34. The word modestly translated here as navel "probably refers to the vulva, coming as it does in sequence after the thighs and before the belly." See Marcia Falk, *Love Lyrics from the Bible: A Translation and Literary Study of the Song of Songs* (Sheffield: Almond Press, 1982), 127–128. See also John F. Craghan, *The Song of Songs and the Book of Wisdom* (Collegeville: The Liturgical Press, 1979), 34.

35. This part of my definition is adapted from J. Dominian, *Christian Marriage* (London: Darton, Longman and Todd, 1968), 243–244.

Chapter Five

1. AAS 56 (1964).

2. DV, 124.

3. Bruce J. Malina, *The New Testament World: Insights from Cultural Anthropology* (Atlanta: John Knox, 1981), 102–103.

4. Ibid., 104.

5. Those who wish to survey the opinions may consult with profit: A. Myre, "Dix ans d'exegese sur le divorce dans le Nouveau Testament," *Le Divorce: l'Eglise catholique ne devrait-elle pas modifier son attitude seculaire a l'egard de l'indissolubilite du mariage* (Montreal:

Fides, 1973), 139–163; J. Fitzmyer, "The Matthean Divorce Texts and Some New Palestinian Evidence," TS 37(1976): 197–226; Bruce Malina, "Does *Porneia* Mean Fornication," *Novum Testamentum* XIV (1972): 10–17; Ernst Haenchen, *The Acts of the Apostles: A Commentary* (Philadelphia: Westminster, 1971), 449; Corrado Marucci, *Parole di Gesu sul divorzio* (Naples: Morcelliana, 1982).

6. Quentin Quesnell, "Made Themselves Eunuchs for the Kingdom of Heaven," CBQ 30 (1968), 349.

7. Bruce J. Malina, *The New Testament World*, 118–121.

8. Theodore Mackin, *Divorce and Remarriage* (New York: Paulist, 1984), 86.

9. *The Apostolic Fathers*, trans. Francis X. Glimm et al. (Washington, D.C.: Catholic University of America Press, 1962), 264.

10. PL 1, 1289.

11. PL 1, 1292.

12. PG 31, 849 and 852.

13. PG 32, 678–679.

14. PG 32, 804–805.

15. Jean Chrysostome, *Virginite*, trans. Bernard Grillet (Paris: Cerf, 1966), 233–237. It is worthwhile to read what he says about marriage throughout this work.

16. PG 61, 154–155.

17. PL 26, 135.

18. Ibid.

19. PL 22, 562.

20. PL 40, 452–453.

21. Ibid., 455.

22. PL 34, 1251.

23. Ibid., 1252. See the same judgment in *De Diversis Quaes-*

tionibus LXXXIII, PL 40,100: "If the Lord admits only fornication as a cause for dismissing a spouse, and does not forbid the dismissal of a pagan spouse, then it follows that paganism is designated as fornication."

24. Ibid., 1253.

25. PL 40, 378.

26. Ibid., 378–379.

27. Ibid., 388.

28. PL 44, 413–474.

29. PL 15, 1765.

30. Ibid., 1766–1767.

31. Ibid., 1767–1768.

32. PL 187, 1407.

33. PL 192, 919.

34. Ibid.

35. PL 187, 1413.

36. Ibid., 1429.

37. DS 1497.

38. DS 1983.

39. DS 1988.

40. See Wilibald Plochl, *Geschichte des Kirchenrechts* (Vienna, 1965), 316–318.

41. See Ladislas Orsy, "Faith, Sacrament, Contract, and Christian Marriage: Disputed Questions," TS 43 (1982), 379–398; Walter Kasper, *Theology of Christian Marriage* (New York: Crossroad, 1981), 78–84.

42. Kevin T. Kelly, *Divorce and Second Marriage: Facing the Challenge* (New York: Seabury, 1983), 39.

43. AAS 33 (1941), 425–426.

44. Cited in Richard A. McCormick, "Notes on Moral Theology," TS 40 (1979), 96, footnote 97.

45. See DS 1807 and footnote. See also Stephen J. Kelleher, *Divorce and Remarriage for Catholics* (New York: Doubleday, 1973), 67; Kevin T. Kelly, *Divorce and Second Marriage*, 87–88.

Afterword

1. International Theological Commission, *Theses on the Relationship Between the Ecclesiastical Magisterium and Theology* (Washington: United States Catholic Conference, 1977), 6.

Selected Bibliography

Achtemeier, Elizabeth R. *The Committed Marriage.* Philadelphia: Westminster, 1976.

Barth, Markus. *Ephesians: Translation and Commentary on Chapters Four to Six.* New York: Doubleday, 1974.

Bassett, William, ed. *The Bond of Marriage: An Ecumenical and Interdisciplinary Study.* Notre Dame: University of Notre Dame Press, 1968.

Bassett, William and Peter Huizing. *The Future of Christian Marriage.* New York: Herder, 1973.

Byron, Brian. "1 Cor. 7:10–15: A Basis for Future Catholic Discipline on Marriage and Divorce." *Theological Studies* 34 (1973), 429–445.

Castillo, Jose M. "No Faith Experience, No Sacramental Event." *Theology Digest* 29 (1981), 37–40.

Cooke, Bernard. *Sacraments and Sacramentality.* Mystic, Conn.: Twenty-Third Publications, 1983.

Cuenin, Walter. *The Marriage of Baptized Non-Believers.* Rome: Gregorian University Press, 1977.

Cuenin, Walter. "Questions: Faith, Sacrament and Law." *Origins,* November 9, 1978, 321–328.

Daube, David. *The Duty of Procreation.* Edinburgh: University Press, 1977.

Dominian, Jack. *Christian Marriage.* London: Darton, Longman and Todd, 1968.

Dominian, Jack. *Marriage, Faith and Love.* New York: Crossroad, 1982.

Doyle, Thomas P., ed. *Marriage Studies: Reflections in Canon Law and Theology,* Volume II, Catholic University of America: Canon Law Society of America, 1982.

Doyle, Thomas P., ed. *Marriage Studies: Reflections in Canon Law and Theology,* Volume III, Catholic University of America: Canon Law Society of America, 1984.

Denneny, Raymond, ed. *Christian Married Love.* San Francisco, Cal.: Ignatius Press, 1981.

Falk, Marcia. *Love Lyrics from the Bible: A translation and Literary Study of the Song of Songs.* Sheffield: Almond Press, 1982.

Fitzmyer, Joseph. "The Matthean Divorce Texts and Some New Palestinian Evidence." *Theological Studies* 37 (1976), 197–226.

Gallagher, Charles A., and others. *Embodied in Love: Sacramental Spirituality and Sexual Intimacy.* New York: Crossroad, 1984.

Gollwitzer, Helmut. *Song of Love: A Biblical Understanding of Sex.* Philadelphia: Fortress, 1979.

Gosling, Justin C. *Marriage and the Love of God.* New York: Sheed and Ward, 1965.

Haring, Bernard. "Rethinking the Sacrament of Matrimony: Excerpt From the Johannine Council." *Catholic World* 197 (1963), 359–65.

Haughton, Rosemary. *Married Love in Christian Life.* London: Burns and Oates, 1965.

Haughton, Rosemary. *The Theology of Marriage.* Notre Dame: Fides, 1971.

Joyce, G.H. *Christian Marriage: An Historical and Doctrinal Study.* London: Sheed and Ward, 1933.

Kasper, Walter. *Theology of Christian Marriage.* New York: Crossroad, 1981.

Kelleher, Stephen J. *Divorce and Remarriage for Catholics.* New York: Doubleday, 1973.

Kelly, Kevin T. *Divorce and Second Marriage: Facing the Challenge.* New York: Seabury, 1983.

Kennedy, Eugene. *What a Modern Catholic Believes about Marriage.* Chicago: Thomas More, 1972.

Kilmartin, Edward. "When is Marriage a Sacrament?" *Theological Studies* 34 (1973), 275–286.

Mackin, Theodore. *What is Marriage?* New York: Paulist, 1982.

Mackin, Theodore. *Divorce and Remarriage*. New York: Paulist, 1984.

Malina, Bruce J. *The New Testament World: Insights from Cultural Anthropology*. Atlanta: John Knox, 1981.

Messenger, E.C. *Two in One Flesh. Part 2: The Mystery of Sex in Marriage*. London: Sands, 1948.

Meyendorff, John. *Marriage: An Orthodox Perspective*. New York: St. Vladimir's Seminary Press, 1978.

Orsy, Ladislas. "Faith, Sacrament, Contract and Christian Marriage: Disputed Questions." *Theological Studies* 43 (1982), 379-398.

Palmer, Paul F. "Christian Marriage: Contract or Covenant?" *Theological Studies* 33 (1972), 617-665.

Palmer, Paul F. "When a Marriage Dies." *America*, Feb. 22, 1975.

Roberts, William P. *Marriage: Sacrament of Hope and Challenge*. Cincinnati: St. Anthony Messenger Press, 1983.

Sampley, J. Paul. *"And the Two Shall Become One Flesh": A Study of Traditions in Ephesians 5:21-33*. Cambridge: University Press, 1971.

Schillebeeckx, Edward. *Marriage: Secular Reality and Saving Mystery*. New York: Sheed and Ward, 1965.

Schmeiser, James A. "Marriage: New Alternatives." *Worship* 55 (1981), 23-33.

Siegle, Bernard Andrew. *Marriage Today*. New York: Alba House, 1973.

Tetlow, Elisabeth M. and Louis M. Tetlow. *Partners in Service: Towards a Biblical Theology of Christian Marriage*. Lanham, Md.: University Press of America, 1983.

Thomas, David M. *Christian Marriage: A Journey Together*. Wilmington: Michael Glazier, 1983.

Vawter, Bruce. "Divorce and the New Testament," *Catholic Biblical Quarterly* 39 (1977), 528-542.

Whelan, Charles M. "Divorced Catholics: A Proposal," *America,* Dec. 7, 1974.

Wrenn, Lawrence G. ed. *Divorce and Remarriage in the Catholic Church.* New York: Newman, 1973.

Young, James J. *Divorcing, Believing, Belonging.* New York: Paulist, 1984.

Young, James J., ed. *Ministering to the Divorced Catholics.* New York: Paulist, 1979.

General Index

Index of Biblical Passages